D0948155

STEPHEN KING

STEPHEN KING

Other titles in the Greenhaven Press Literary
Companion to Contemporary Authors series:

Tom Clancy
Michael Crichton
John Grisham
J.K. Rowling

The Greenhaven Press
LITERARY COMPANION
to Contemporary Authors

STEPHEN KING

Karin Coddon, *Book Editor*

Daniel Leone, *President*
Bonnie Szumski, *Publisher*
Scott Barbour, *Managing Editor*

**GREENHAVEN
PRESS®**

THOMSON

GALE

San Diego • Detroit • New York • San Francisco • Cleveland
New Haven, Conn. • Waterville, Maine • London • Munich

THOMSON

GALE

For more information, contact
Greenhaven Press   **03-04**
27500 Drake Rd.
Farmington Hills, MI 48331-3535
Or you can visit our Internet site at http://www.gale.com

LIBRARY OF CONGRESS CATALOGING-IN-PUBLICATION DATA

Readings on Stephen King / Karin Coddon, book editor.
    p. cm. — (The Greenhaven Press literary companion to contemporary authors)
    Includes bibliographical references and index.
    ISBN 0-7377-1666-5 (lib. bdg. : alk. paper) —
    ISBN 0-7377-1667-3 (pbk. : alk. paper)
        1. King, Stephen, 1947– . 2. Novelists, American—20th century—Biography.
    3. Horror tales, American—History and criticism. I. Coddon, Karin S. (Karin Susan)
    II. Series.
    PS3561.I483Z83 2004
    813'.54—dc21   2003049125
    [B]

Printed in the United States of America

Contents

Chapter 1: Stephen King, Portrait of the Artist

Chapter 2: Overarching Themes and Conventions in King's Fiction

Chapter 3: Reading the Books

rabid dog Cujo, Donna demonstrates courage in facing problems both ordinary and extraordinary.

FOREWORD

Contemporary authors who earn millions of dollars writing best-sellers often face criticism that their work cannot be taken seriously as literature. For example, throughout most of his career, horror writer Stephen King has been dismissed by literary critics as a "hack" who writes grisly tales that appeal to the popular taste of the masses. Similarly, the extremely popular Harry Potter books by J.K. Rowling have been criticized as a clever marketing phenomenon that lack the imagination and depth of classic works of literature. Whether these accusations are accurate, however, remains debatable. As romance novelist Jayne Ann Krentz has pointed out:

> Popular fiction has been around forever but rarely has it been viewed as important in and of itself. Rarely have we acknowledged that it has a crucial place in culture. . . . The truth is, popular fiction—mysteries, science fiction, sword and sorcery, fantasy, glitz, romance, historical saga, horror, techno-thrillers, legal thrillers, forensic medical thrillers, serial killer thrillers, westerns, etc.—popular fiction is its own thing. It stands on its own. It draws its power from the ancient heroic traditions of storytelling—not modern angst. It is important, even if it is entertaining.

Although its importance often goes unrecognized, popular fiction has the power to reach millions of readers and to thus influence culture and society. The medium has the potential to shape culture because of the large and far-flung audience that is drawn to read these works. As a result of their large readership, contemporary authors have a unique venue in which to reflect and explore the social and political issues that they find important. Far from being mere escapist fiction, their works often address topics that challenge readers to consider their perspectives on current and universal themes. For example, Michael Crichton's novel *Jurassic Park*, while an entertaining if disturbing story about what could happen if dinosaurs roamed the planet today, also explores the potential negative consequences of scientific advances and the ethical issues of DNA experimentation. Similarly, in his 1994 novel *Disclosure*, Crichton tells the story of a man who suffers predatory sexual harassment by his female supervisor. By reversing the expected genders of the victim and aggressor, Crichton added fuel to the debate over sexual politics in the workplace.

Some works of fiction are compelling and popular because they address specific concerns that are prevalent in a culture at a given time. For example, John Grisham has written numerous novels about the theme of corruption in America's oldest legal and business institutions. In books such as *The Firm* and *The Pelican Brief*, courageous though sometimes naive individuals must confront established, authoritarian systems at great personal danger in order to bring the truth to light. Written at a time when government and corporate scandals dominated the headlines, his novels reflect a faith in the power of the individual to achieve justice.

In an era when 98 percent of American households have a television and annual video sales outnumber book sales, it is impossible to ignore the fact that popular fiction also inspires people to read. The Harry Potter stories have been enormously popular with both adults and children, setting records on the *New York Times* best-seller lists. Stephen King's books, which have never gone out of print, frequently occupy four to five shelves in bookstores and libraries. Although literary critics may find fault with some works of popular fiction, record numbers of people are finding value in reading these contemporary authors whose stories hold meaning for them and which shape popular culture.

Greenhaven Press's Literary Companion to Contemporary Authors series is designed to provide an introduction to the works of modern authors. Each volume profiles a different author. A biographical essay sets the stage by tracing the author's life and career. Next, each anthology in the series contains a varied selection of essays that express diverse views on the author under discussion. A concise introduction that presents the contributing writers' main themes and insights accompanies each selection. Essays, profiles, and reviews offer in-depth biographical information, analysis of the author's predominant themes, and literary analysis of the author's trademark books. In addition, primary sources such as interviews and the author's own essays and writings are included wherever possible. A comprehensive index and an annotated table of contents help readers quickly locate material of interest. In order to facilitate further research, each title includes a bibliography of the author's works and books about the author's writing and life. These features make Greenhaven Press's Literary Companion to Contemporary Authors series ideal for readers interested in literary analysis on the world's modern authors and works.

Introduction: The Horror in Everyday Life

Stephen King is one of the most commercially successful novelists in the world, the author of more than thirty best-selling books of fiction, translated into thirty-two different languages. With the exception of *Rage*, which was withdrawn from publication at King's request, all of his books remain in print, an impressive feat for an author whose first book appeared in 1974. King's vast and enduring popularity is testimonial to the richness of his work, which attracts a remarkably loyal—yet also remarkably diverse—readership.

Different readers find different pleasures in King's fiction. Some, certainly, read King for the sheer escapism offered by his well-crafted, often intricate plots, realistic characters, and epic themes such as the struggle between good and evil. The thrill of a good make-believe scare also has an enduring appeal. Many of King's fans are avid readers of other popular contemporary horror and fantasy writers such as Clive Barker, Dean Koontz, Bentley Little, and Anne Rice. But King's "crossover appeal" also attracts readers who might ordinarily have little interest in monsters, extraterrestrials, and hauntings. These readers are drawn to King's themes of ordinary people facing extraordinary yet universal crises: the horrible inexorability of death *(Pet Sematary)*, the social alienation of those deemed "different" *(Carrie, It, Rage)*, and the powerlessness of individuals against tyrannical forces *(Firestarter, The Stand)*.

King's reputation as a "serious" writer continues to grow, with more critics attending to his treatment of complex philosophical themes and discussing his place in a long literary tradition. But the debate over whether King is a writer for the ages should not obscure the fact that he is emphatically a writer for a particular time and place: contemporary America. King's cultural and historical specificity is registered in his often pointed social critique. The crass materialism of *Needful Things* satirizes America's commodity culture, in which the purchase of a desirable item—whether a rare baseball card or piece of Elvis memorabilia—seems to promise the buyer bliss. The lethal political agendas in *The Stand* and *The Dead Zone* and the ruthless CIA-like operations of "The Shop" in *Firestarter* and *The Tommyknockers* reflect post-Vietnam, post-Watergate mistrust of the government and public officials, whose motives King represents as self-serving and amoral. The "family values" that virtually all American politicians claim to defend are transformed in the world of Stephen King to a flimsy veneer that barely conceals dysfunction, conflict, and, often, domestic violence.

Even when King's satire is playful, his underlying social criticism is sharp. Small-town bullies drive cars with Reagan bumper stickers, suggesting an association between blind prejudice and right-wing American politics. The antismoking advocates who resort to murderous "behavioral modifications" evoke the overzealousness of modern self-help movements. The technological "magic" of the computer age contrasts with the dissatisfaction of contemporary family life as an unhappy husband presses the "Delete" key on his computer to rid himself of his shrewish wife and obnoxious headbanger son.

Thus despite all the supernatural trappings of his work, King is at heart of *this* world. "I am always going to be a social novelist," he observed in the mid-1980s to critic Douglas E. Winter:

> I am a social creature; I am a creature of my time. The consistent beat that comes through a lot of the reviews is my use of brand names, and the "mass-cult" surface of my novels. But that's because these things are part of my

life, and because I refuse to deny either my times or my interest in my times. . . . I am also interested in people who interact on a smaller social and political framework—particularly that of the family. The social ethics of the family. The individual.[1]

The monsters, ghosts, and maniacs who haunt King's various "nightmares and dreamscapes" occupy familiar terrain: Disney World and Las Vegas, the family hearth and classic roadster, the small towns and two-lane highways traversed by innocuous yet strangely menacing tanker trucks. The ultimate power of King's imaginative vision, then, may lie less in the supernatural creatures that terrorize his protagonists and keep his readers awake late at night, and more in his recognition of the potential for horror to impose itself, unbidden and with little warning, onto ordinary, contemporary American existence.

1. Quoted in Douglas E. Winter, *Stephen King: The Art of Darkness*. New York: New American Library, 1984, pp. 84–85.

STEPHEN KING: A BIOGRAPHY

It is at their own risk that readers—and critics—of fiction look to the particular events of any author's life to find an enhanced understanding of his or her work. By definition novelists traffic in the imagination. This is especially true of those who write about the supernatural. Nonetheless, the ordinary experiences of everyday life may provide the raw materials for fictive worlds—even those fantastic ones created by Stephen King. As King himself has said, "I write fantasies, but draw from the world I see."[1] Indeed, King's novels and stories are remarkable even in the genres of horror and fantasy for their characteristic juxtapositions of mundane small-town life and paranormal terror, of ordinary, plainspoken people (frequently northern New Englanders) confronting extraordinary monsters, whether from beyond the grave, outer space, or their own government.

CHILDHOOD AND FAMILY

An examination of the life of Stephen King provides no definitive answer to one of his most frequently asked questions: "Where do you get your ideas?" However, by King's own admission, elements of his childhood and early youth influenced his development as a writer and laid the groundwork for his later thematic fascination with family dysfunction, youthful innocence and youthful brutality, social injustice and the plight of "outsiders," the stubbornness of hope, and the inexorability of evil.

Stephen Edwin King was born in Portland, Maine, on September 21, 1947, to Donald Edwin and Nellie Ruth Pillsbury

King, who also had an adopted son, David, two years older than Stephen. One night, when Stephen was around two, his father announced that he was going out to buy a pack of cigarettes and walked away from the family forever. Nellie King, forced into the unenviable position of sole breadwinner for herself and two young sons, took a series of low-paying jobs across New England and (briefly) in Fort Wayne, Indiana. She eventually resettled her family in Durham, Maine, where Nellie's elderly, frail parents resided, in 1958.

King's childhood, perhaps because as well as in spite of the family's economic hardships and frequent moves, afforded the boy areas of pleasurable escapism. An avid reader, young King started writing, mostly science fiction and adventure stories, at seven years old; by twelve he was submitting his tales to magazines, though with no success. He and his brother, David, got hold of an old printing press and began to publish (mainly for their own entertainment) a newspaper called "Dave's Rag." "Dave's Rag" unofficially became the first publication in which King's fiction would appear.

A FATHER'S UNEXPECTED LEGACY

At around twelve or thirteen, King made a momentous discovery: In the attic of his aunt and uncle's home he found a cache of his father's old books. Donald King, according to Nellie, had himself been a failed writer, and his tastes decidedly ran to horror and fantasy. Among the discoveries in the attic were books by H.G. Wells and pulp magazine collections of horror writing. Coupled with young King's love for the "B" sci-fi movies popular in the late 1950s and early 1960s, the revelation of his vanished father's literary tastes seemed to cement the youth's aspirations to be a successful writer of the dark and fantastic. Soon, King was reading modern masters of the supernatural genre—Ray Bradbury, Richard Matheson, Fritz Leiber, Robert Bloch, and Shirley Jackson—along with Edgar Allan Poe and H.P. Lovecraft.

King's literary development continued through high

school in Lisbon, Maine; he and best friend Chris Chesley self-published a collection of their stories in 1963. Socially, the adolescent King was introverted, on the outside of the macho "jock culture" that often determines teenage popularity and peer acceptance. King has commented extensively on the influence his adolescence had regarding his sympathy for his alienated teen protagonists in *Carrie*, *Rage*, and *Christine*, among other works:

> My stories of adolescent violence were all drawn, in some degree, from my own memories of high school. That particular truth, as I recalled it when writing as an adult, was unpleasant enough. I remember high school as a time of misery and resentment. In Iroquois trials of manhood, naked warriors were sent running down a gauntlet of braves swinging clubs and jabbing with the butt ends of spears. In high school the goal is Graduation Day instead of a manhood feather, and the weapons are replaced by insults, slights, and epithets, many of them racial, but I imagine the feelings are about the same. The victims aren't always naked, and yet a good deal of the rawest hazing does take place on playing fields and in locker rooms, where the marks are thinly dressed or not dressed at all. The locker room is where *Carrie* starts, with girls throwing sanitary napkins at a sexually ignorant girl who thinks she is bleeding to death. . . . I don't trust people who look back on high school with fondness; too many of them were part of the overclass, those who were taunters instead of tauntees.[2]

Nonetheless, King's high school years ended on a decidedly promising note: In 1965, his story "I Was a Teenage Grave Robber" was accepted for publication by *Comics Review*. The high school outcast was now an officially published writer.

COLLEGE TRANSFORMATIONS

As he neared high school graduation, King was also working on a novel then called *Getting It On* (later retitled *Rage*), an edgy tale of teenage alienation centering on a young man who shoots his teacher and holds his classmates hostage. *Rage* was finally published in 1977 as the first of several books appearing under King's pseudonym "Richard Bachman." Later, in the 1990s, *Rage* would prove to be the source of much grief to King when it, arguably, seemed to have inspired several teenage school shootings. King ultimately asked his publisher to remove the book from print, and has referred to it as the one book he regrets publishing.

Despite all its later notoriety, *Rage* was not the sole novel King was working on as he prepared to enter college, on scholarship, at the University of Maine, Orono. *The Long Walk*, also to appear later as a "Bachman book," was completed during King's freshman year in Orono. King's writerly self-confidence was shattered when Random House rejected the book with a cursory form letter. However, the same year he sold his first story for money; for "The Glass Floor," *Startling Mystery Stories* paid King all of $35.

King's college years constituted a period of striking personal as well as professional development. In 1966 he arrived at Orono, a small-town, conservative Methodist youth who was a registered Republican and accepted without question his government's Vietnam policy. Soon, however, King's social conscience, already stirred by growing up in a poor single-parent family, was roused anew by the campus antiwar movement. The importance of King's political awakening has often been understated, yet the strong undercurrent of liberal social values throughout his work (not to mention his frequent tweaking of Republicans) no doubt owes much to his formative experiences at Orono. In his middle age King would ruefully quote the seminal 1960s counterculture movie *Easy Rider* in referring to the lost hopes of his generation: "There was a time when we had it in our hands and were within a few months or three or four marches of literally changing this country. . . . We blew it."[3] Nevertheless, King's satirical critique of consumerism in *Needful Things*, his sinister portraits of government secrecy and amoral experimentation in *Firestarter* and *The Stand* and of right-wing antiabortion fanatics in *Insomnia*, and perhaps even his dubbing his secular Antichrist "Randall *Flagg*" all testify to the intertwining of the supernatural, the social, and the political in King's worldview that was surfacing during his college years.

At Orono, the prolific literary output that would come to mark King as a successful novelist was already discernable. He wrote fiction, poetry, and an antiestablishment column called "King's Garbage Truck" that appeared in the college newspaper, the *Maine Campus*. As an English major, King studied a traditional curriculum, and was most drawn to the great naturalist novelists, including Thomas Hardy, Theodore Dreiser, and Jack London. "Their stories would suggest to me that almost everything we do has a history," he observed to Douglas Winter. "No matter where you come in on any situation, you are not coming in at the beginning."[4] Naturalistic writers emphasized a realistic, almost scientific representation of human experience and the relative impotence of free will against forces beyond an individual's control. King's use of naturalistic style, setting, and character in constructing tales of the supernatural contrasts with the traditionally ornate language, eerie surroundings, and romanticized heroes and villains traditionally employed by horror writers, from Mary Shelley and Bram Stoker to Anne Rice. However, King's creative writing received a mixed reception from his professors; some, like Burton Hatlen and Ted Holmes, were enthusiastic boosters of the young writer's talents, while others were less than impressed by his choice of subject matter, which was not deemed sufficiently literary or "serious." The skepticism from highbrow critics both within and outside of academia would taunt King for much of his career. Nonetheless, King's instructors thought highly enough of him to allow him as an undergraduate the unprecedented privilege of coteaching a course in popular American literature.

THE STRUGGLING FAMILY MAN AND WRITER

During King's senior year he met a junior named Tabitha Spruce, who was also an aspiring writer from a working-class background. Although Tabitha Spruce's initial impression of King was of a hippie in dire need of a haircut, the two soon became close. "All he cared about was getting everything he could out of school and writing his head off,"[5] Tabitha later recalled. In 1971, midway through Tabitha's senior year, the couple married; their first child, Naomi, was born not long after.

The young family struggled, much as King's mother had during his childhood. King taught high school English at the Hampden Academy in Hermon, Maine, but his salary was insufficient to support a household that soon included a second child, Joe. The family lived in a rented trailer; King used its small furnace room to type out his fiction on an Olivetti manual typewriter. By this time King had sold several short stories to various men's magazines, but he was also amassing rejection slips, along with bills. Doubleday had rejected both *Getting It On* and *The Running Man*, although not without offering some encouragement from editor William G. Thompson. King was not only disheartened by the rejections but also increasingly overtaxed by his family's ongoing financial woes. In addition to his teaching, he took on part-time jobs at a gas station and a dry cleaners (the latter would inspire his eerie short story "The Mangler."). Suffering from exhauston, the effects of heavy alcohol consumption, and discouragement, King also found himself afflicted by writer's block. His plans for an epic fantasy novel about a gunslinger (which would eventually result in his *Dark Tower* series) went on hold.

Yet King's creativity, although blunted by hard luck and overwork, would not be repressed. In the winter of 1972 he forced himself to tinker with a short story he had written the previous summer, hoping to hone the manuscript into suitable shape for submission to *Cavalier*, one of the men's magazines in which he had placed other works. Based loosely on

King's own unpleasant high school experiences and on memories of an outcast female teen who lived near his family in Durham, *Carrie* very nearly never made its way to finished form. King grew discouraged and tossed the incomplete manuscript into a trash can, where it was salvaged by his wife. Tabitha King read the manuscript, liked it, and urged her husband to return to his revisions. All the same, King held out no great hopes for *Carrie*'s success: "My considered opinion was that I had written the world's all-time loser,"[6] he admits. Once again, he submitted the manuscript to William G. Thompson at Doubleday, the editor who had responded positively to his previous (although ultimately rejected) work.

CARRIE CHANGES KING'S FORTUNES

This time, Thompson offered more than simple encouragement. At the editor's urging King revised the novel's last fifty pages, after which Doubleday purchased the novel, in March 1973, for an advance of $2,500. Thompson had to telegram the author with the good news; the Kings were in such dire financial straits that they had had their telephone disconnected. When paperback rights to *Carrie* were sold two months later to New American Library for $400,000, the Kings were incredulous—and ecstatic. King recollects, "It was a great feeling of liberation, because I was free at last to quit teaching and fulfill what I believe is my only function in life: to write books. Good, bad, or indifferent books, that's for others to decide; it's enough to *write*."[7] The family soon moved to North Windham, a small town near Portland, Maine, but King's first great success was bittersweet. His beloved mother, Nellie, died of cancer before *Carrie* appeared in print.

Although a modest success in hardcover, *Carrie* initially sold more than 1 million copies in paperback. King's second novel, *'Salem's Lot*, a reimagining of Bram Stoker's classic vampire tale set in rural Maine, followed in 1975. A year later, the movie version of *Carrie*, starring Sissy Spacek and directed by Brian DePalma, was a surprise hit, spiking sales of the original novel as well as the newly released paperback version of *'Salem's Lot.* DePalma's film inaugurated the first of many successful movie versions of King's novels, compounding his fame and "brand-name" status. *The Shining,* inspired by a visit to the historic Stanley Hotel in Estes Park, Colorado, appeared in 1977 and was King's first hardcover best-seller. It too would spawn a successful movie, although King made little secret of his disappointment in Stanley Kubrick's 1980 treatment of his work, which subordinated the supernatural elements to the psychological (perhaps most famously embodied by Jack Nicholson's over-the-top, maniacal performance as he wields an ax and taunts, "Heeeeeeere's Johnny!"). Other King novels and stories became films as well, with mixed results. King's film adaptations ranged from the Oscar-caliber *Shawshank Redemption, Stand by Me, Misery, Dolores Claiborne,* and *The Green Mile* to the comparatively low-budget pulp horror of *Creepshow, Firestarter, Christine,* and *Pet Sematary.* King frequently appeared in small parts in the movies, including the notorious flop *Maximum Overdrive,* which he also directed.

King's strictly literary output in the decade or so following *Carrie* was little short of mind-boggling. He wrote novels of classic horror, including *The Stand, The Dead Zone, It,* and *Pet Sematary;* the first of the fantasy *Dark Tower* series; *The Talisman,* his first collaboration with Peter Straub; two collections of short stories; and a nonfiction work on the modern horror genre titled *Danse Macabre.* His prolific output prompted critical derision, as did his plain writing style and fantastic subject matter. Although King has sardonically referred to himself as "Bestsellasaurus Rex" and "the literary equivalent of a Big Mac," his failure to garner literary respect was becoming a long-standing thorn in his side. Yet with each new work, his style and thematic range continued to develop as he made use of everyday language and pop-culture allusions, small-town Maine settings, and explicitly

American families in late-twentieth-century turmoil.

But the pressures of massive fame and fortune took a toll on King. His consumption of alcohol and cocaine was increasing to the extent that he later admitted to having little memory of even writing his novel *Cujo* (published in 1981). Reminiscent of Gard, the alcoholic poet with his hidden bottles and embarrassing public scenes in *The Tommyknockers* (first drafted in 1983), King was even resorting to gulping alcohol-laced cough medicine until his wife led some family friends in a successful intervention. King would later speak and write candidly about his addictions, emphatically rejecting the romantic notion that artists are characteristically prone to self-destruction and substance abuse.

KING'S GROWTH AS AN ARTIST

King's creative productivity and commercial success continued throughout the 1980s and 1990s. Although *Different Seasons*, which inspired the two highly acclaimed, "serious" films *Stand by Me* and *The Shawshank Redemption*, marked his first foray into nonsupernatural fiction, he also broke new ground with several full-length novels with *Misery, Gerald's Game, Dolores Claiborne*, and *Rose Madder*. Interestingly, three of these four novels focus on abused but gutsy women terrorized less by supernatural forces than by spousal brutality. While King's identification of the horror inherent in the dysfunctionality of the American family is a major theme throughout his work, his excursions into the psychological terror born of domestic violence sparked a debate among critics about the extent and sincerity of King's sympathies with feminism. King himself shrugged off the label of "feminist writer," but there seems little doubt that the examples of his late mother and of Tabitha King, an accomplished novelist in her own right and her husband's favorite reader and critic, influenced his depictions of multidimensional, courageous heroines. The critical tide started to shift—at least in some venues—in favor of King. His short fiction was appearing regularly in the venerable *New Yorker* magazine; his story "The Man in the Black Suit" won the prestigious 1996 O. Henry award; and his growing following among academics resulted in the publication of several books of serious King literary criticism, as well as his work's frequent inclusion in college curricula.

KING'S BRUSH WITH DEATH

Despite the success of his nonsupernatural work and the grudging critical respect it was garnering, King did not abandon horror fiction, continuing to publish novels (*Desperation, Insomnia, Bag of Bones*), short fiction (*Four Past Midnight, Nightmares and Dreamscapes*), and screenplays and teleplays (including the made-for-TV *Rose Red*, a miniseries of *The Stand*, and an episode of *The X-Files*). He also continued his collaborations with Peter Straub and his fantasy *Dark Tower* series. He began to experiment with new modes of marketing as well; *The Green Mile* was originally published as a six-part serial novel, and "Riding the Bullet" first appeared as an e-book available only on the Internet.

In June 1999 King's life changed dramatically when he was struck by a van as he was taking a stroll near his summer home in rural Maine. King's injuries were grave—they included a collapsed lung, broken ribs, a broken leg, and a fractured hip—and required three weeks of hospitalization, several surgeries, and months of painful rehabilitation. Of his four postaccident books—the nonfiction *On Writing, Dreamcatcher*, the short story collection *Everything's Eventual*, and *From a Buick 8*—all but the anthology, which features stories largely composed before 1999, reflect his recent ordeal. Two major characters in *Dreamcatcher* and *From a Buick 8* are seriously injured in traffic accidents (one fatally), and in *On Writing*, begun prior to the accident, King addresses the matter directly. Perhaps not coincidentally, although King has denied any explicit connection, the author told *Entertainment Weekly* in the fall of 2002 that he intends to cease writing for publication (although with a caveat that a last installment of the *Dark Tower* series remains in the offing).

STEPHEN KING, "REGULAR GUY"

Though most fans prefer not to contemplate a time when a new work from the master of modern horror does not appear every year or two, King's possible retirement from publication is not likely to entail a complete retreat from public life. The onetime antiwar radical has been in his maturity an ardent supporter of literacy programs and an opponent of censorship. Both Stephen and Tabitha King have made appearances for local Democratic political candidates and publicly decried proposed state legislation to strike down antidiscrimination laws for gays. In the early 1990s King was able to combine his sense of civic responsibility with his lifelong love of baseball, donating $1 million for a new Little League field in Bangor, Maine. The *Bangor Daily News* wrote in praise of Stephen and Tabitha King's philanthropy, which also included a major donation to the Old Town Public Library: "Coming out of a decade when the objective of having money was to hoard it and flaunt it, it is refreshing to see authors Stephen and Tabitha King dealing with wealth the old-fashioned way: They have earned it, and they have chosen to share it."[8]

With their three children—Naomi, Joe, and Owen—grown, Stephen and Tabitha King divide their time between their homes in Maine and Florida. Their famed gothic Victorian mansion in Bangor has, unfortunately, proven a magnet for some of King's more obsessive fans. In 1991 a crazed fan named Erik Keene broke in to the house and threatened Tabitha, who was at home alone, with a bomb he falsely claimed to possess. Like many celebrities, King has had to cope with unwanted, even dangerous, public attention and the loss of his privacy. Yet he has said, "I don't want to live like Michael Jackson or like Elvis did at Graceland. That's gross."[9] King's determination to live like a "regular guy"—indeed, the kind of ordinary small-town Maine fellow he has so frequently written of—is perhaps best exemplified by his membership in a rock band with fellow writers Dave Barry, Amy Tan, Roy Blount, Ridley Pearson, and a revolving cast of other frustrated rock 'n' rollers. Although Barry has quipped that the band, called the Rock Bottom Remainders after a publishing term for unsold books, "plays music as well as Metallica writes novels,"[10] the group has performed at booksellers' conventions, clubs, and charity events, once even sharing a London stage with Bruce Springsteen.

After nearly three decades as the preeminent modern horror writer, King has shown no signs of exhausting his talent. Regardless of whether he chooses to continue sharing his fiction with his admiring public, his unique contributions to contemporary American writing and his expansion of the popular literary imagination secure his legacy. Like his forebears Mary Shelley, Bram Stoker, and Edgar Allan Poe, each of whose work was at one time critically dismissed as "mere" horror fiction, King will be both enjoyed and studied for the ages.

NOTES

1. From Stephen King's Keynote Address, Vermont Library Conference, VEMA, annual meeting, May 26, 1999.

2. From King's Keynote Address, Vermont Library Conference.

3. Quoted in "Stephen King Day Revisits '60s, '70s," *Bangor Daily News*, October 4, 2001.

4. Quoted in Douglas E. Winter, *Stephen King: The Art of Darkness*. New York: New American Library, 1984, p. 21.

5. Quoted in Winter, *Stephen King*, p. 23.

6. Quoted in George Beahm, *Stephen King: America's Best-Loved Boogeyman*. Kansas City, MO: Andrews McMeel, 1998, p. 27.

7. Quoted in Beahm, *Stephen King*, p. 30.

8. Quoted in Beahm, *Stephen King*, p. 175.

9. Quoted in Beahm, *Stephen King*, p. 147.

10. Quoted in Beahm, *Stephen King*, p. 170.

CHAPTER 1

Stephen King, Portrait of the Artist

READINGS ON
STEPHEN KING

Stephen King: Celebrity Writer or Modern Master?

George Beahm

George Beahm is among the leading authorities on Stephen King, and is the author of *The Stephen King Companion*, *The Stephen King Encyclopedia*, and *Stephen King: America's Best-Loved Boogeyman*, from which the following selection is excerpted. Beahm argues that King's celebrity and prolific output have tended to overshadow his genuine talent as a writer. According to Beahm, literary critics have not only denigrated King but also appear oblivious to the growing academic interest in his fiction. However, King has slowly begun to gain recognition from the literary establishment, as evidenced by his publication in the *New Yorker* magazine, his O. Henry prize for short fiction, and the laudatory words of Joyce Carol Oates, one of the country's most respected novelists. Such shifting opinions are reminders of the capriciousness of literary tastes. However, Beahm acknowledges that only time will determine King's ultimate literary legacy. For the present, it is clear to Beahm that King's work has already left a mark on the popular imagination.

Every year in November, book publishers around the world gather in Frankfurt, Germany, to get a preview of the big books for sale, most of them from the United States. In contrast to previous years, however, 1997's offerings seemed pretty ordinary—business as usual—until rumors began to fly that Stephen King, after two decades with NAL [New American Library], was shopping around *Bag of Bones*, his latest novel.

George Beahm, *Stephen King: America's Best-Loved Boogeyman*. Kansas City, MO: Andrews McMeel, 1998. Copyright © 1998 by George W. Beahm. Reproduced by permission of the publisher.

The rumors, as it turned out, were founded in truth. King was splitting from NAL in a very publicized divorce, to the chagrin of the publishing industry and King himself, engineered by King's agent and manager, Arthur B. Greene.

King, however, was nowhere to be found. In fact, he was halfway around the world, out of touch, unavailable for comment, just as he wished.

A winter of King's discontent, the best-selling author looking for a new home was getting a reception from other publishers fit for a king—for *the* Stephen King, who got $2,500 for *Carrie* in 1974 and was now asking $17 million for *Bag of Bones*.

KING AS CELEBRITY AUTHOR

King, who started out as a writer, then became a major figure in popular culture, inevitably became a celebrity. The average guy on the street, when pigeonholed, will probably not have read any of King's books, though he might have seen a movie or two, but he will know the household name—Stephen King.

The Stephen King Phenomenon, as Michael Collings termed it, is unique among his fellow scriveners. The other best-selling storytellers—Tom Clancy, Michael Crichton, John Grisham, Patricia Cornwell, Dean Koontz, and Anne Rice, to name a few—have sold millions of copies of their books, and their reputations rest largely on their annual blockbusters.

King not only sells millions of books and belongs in that rank but he belongs in another rank, as well: a prolific *writer.* Working steadily, four hours a day, King creates a torrent of words—letters to the local newspaper, op-ed pieces, poetry, nonfiction in all lengths, screenplays, short stories, novellas, and, of course, monstrous-sized novels that make his publishers and his readers happy, while distressing some of his book critics, particularly those who have literary airs and look down at King, whom they perceive as a horror writer, the print equivalent of Jordy Verrill (a Maine hayseed portrayed by King in *Creepshow*).

King, back in his college days, decided the distinction between popular and literary fiction was arbitrary and consciously set out to bridge that gap.

For years, the literary cognoscenti have overlooked the fact that well-regarded academicians, gathering for the Literature of the Fantastic conferences, read papers on King's fiction, taking it seriously.

KING AND THE LITERARY ESTABLISHMENT

In recent years, however, the critical perception has shifted ever so slightly: King not only was the subject of a weekend seminar at his alma mater, where critical papers were delivered, but he started appearing regularly in the august pages of *The New Yorker* magazine, premiering with a long essay, "Head Down," selected for inclusion in an anthology of best sports writing that year; and, more recently, "The Man in the Black Suit," which not only won an award inside the fantasy field but, more significantly, *outside* it: The story took first place in the *Prize Stories 1996: The O. Henry Awards*, beating out a thousand other eligible stories, including the usual bumper crop of fiction by literary writers, some of whom were likely self-righteously pissed that King—vocal in his condemnation of the literary establishment—had even made an appearance in the book.

King, not his critics, has a right to be upset. His name is often used—misused, actually—as an example of a writer whose work can't be good because he's popular. (King, who has categorically stated that he thinks he'll never win a National Book Award, decided that a few years ago, in the company of other best-selling popular writers, he'd make an appearance at one of their award ceremonies; so he bought a table and invited his friend John Grisham and others who joined him in a show of protest, probably to the horror of the other attendees. This was *their* party, the literary writers probably sneered, and how *dare* these, these popular novelists make a mockery of our awards ceremony! Do they think *they* are going to win anything here? Not bloody likely!)

KING'S TALENT VALIDATES HIS POPULARITY

In the end, all that matters is the writing—a fact that some of the literary critics conveniently overlook, as they dismiss him.

In the end, it gets down to what King puts on paper. The fans, the adulation, the articles and books written about him, the interviews and endless profiles, the media attention, the cult of the celebrity—none of that matters. Only the words matter; the rest is eyewash.

On April 16, 1997, at Princeton University, one of its professors—who, not coincidentally, happens to be in the first rank of American literary writers—introduced King at a public talk. She said:

> Like all great writers of Gothic horror, King is both a storyteller and an inventor of startling images and metaphors, which linger long in the memory and would seem to spring from a collective unconscious and thoroughly domestic American soil. His fellow writers admire him for his commitment to the craft of fiction and the generosity of his involvement in the literary community.

The speaker who introduced him was Joyce Carol Oates, a writer and academic who, in my opinion, deserves a nomination, if not the office, of First Lady of Literary Fiction.

What, then, does it say when she endorses King and sings his praises? Does it mean she's lost all control of her critical faculties?

It means, in short, *pay attention!* There's something here, folks. Look past the boogeyman's fright mask and dig deeper, and you'll see stories like "The Body" and "Rita Hayworth and Shawshank Redemption," "The Reach," "The Woman in the Room," "The Last Rung on the Ladder," *Misery, The Green Mile,* and "The Man in the Black Suit."

THE WRITER'S VOICE

King can write.

As King told *Fangoria* magazine, "People don't read me because they want horror. They read me because they like Stephen King. I've come to that conclusion over the years. . . . I think they come back for the voice, more than anything else."

That voice sounds out loud and clear, speaking to millions of readers and, through his movies, many millions more. King, who celebrated his fiftieth birthday on September 21, 1997, can look back and take pride in his still-growing body of work, which, when taken together, gives a unique view of contemporary America in a way that is refreshingly original and compulsively readable. Let the future decide King's place in Maine literature or American literature.

The Influence of a Cold War Childhood on Stephen King's Imagination

Stephen King

Stephen King's 1981 nonfiction book *Danse Macabre* is chiefly concerned with modern horror, focusing on fiction, folklore, television, and especially "B" science fiction movies from the 1950s and 1960s. However, King grounds his discussion in his own experiences as a young boy and aspiring writer growing up in turbulent post–World War II America. In the following selection from *Danse Macabre*'s opening chapter, King recalls a moment from his childhood in which a Saturday afternoon showing of *Earth vs. the Flying Saucers* (1957) was interrupted by the theater manager's announcement that the Russians had beaten the United States into outer space with the successful launching of the satellite *Sputnik I*.

For King, the experience seemed like a collision between the fantasy threat of martian invaders and the paranoid realities of the Cold War, in which the United States and Russia were engaged in an unnerving technology race to conquer outer space and to develop nuclear weapons. Like many of his generation, King sees parallels between the popularity of alien-invaders movies and 1950s Cold War anxieties. This atmosphere of technological revolution and nuclear jitters, fantasy space invaders and ominous Russian satellites, created for the young Stephen King "fertile ground for the seeds of terror." Certainly the incident in the Stratford Theater left a lasting impression on the young boy's imagination. The deadly alien invasions of *The Tommyknockers* and *Dreamcatcher*, the malevolent gov-

Stephen King, *Danse Macabre*. New York: Everest House, 1981. Copyright © 1981 by Stephen King. Reproduced by permission.

ernment entities in *Firestarter* and *The Stand*, and even
the B-movie werewolf that terrorizes a twelve-year-old boy
in *It* all echo King's discovery of "real terror" described in
this anecdote about one afternoon in 1957.

For me, the terror—the real terror, as opposed to whatever
demons and boogeys which might have been living in my own
mind—began on an afternoon in October of 1957. I had just
turned ten. And, as was only fitting, I was in a movie theater:
the Stratford Theater in downtown Stratford, Connecticut.

TWO PHILOSOPHIES OF TERROR

The movie that day was and is one of my all-time favorites,
and the fact that it—rather than a Randolph Scott western
or a John Wayne war movie—was playing was also only fitting. The Saturday matinee on that day when the real terror
began was *Earth vs. the Flying Saucers*, starring Hugh Marlowe, who at the time was perhaps best known for his role as
Patricia Neal's jilted and rabidly xenophobic boyfriend in
The Day the Earth Stood Still—a slightly older and altogether
more rational science fiction movie.

In *The Day the Earth Stood Still*, an alien named Klaatu
(Michael Rennie in a bright white intergalactic leisure suit)
lands on The Mall in Washington, D.C., in a flying saucer
(which, when under power, glows like one of those plastic Je-
suses they used to give out at Vacation Bible School for mem-
orizing Bible verses). Klaatu strides down the gangway and
pauses there at the foot, the focus of every horrified eye and
the muzzles of several hundred Army guns. It is a moment of
memorable tension, a moment that is sweet in retrospect—
the sort of moment that makes people like me simple movie
fans for life. Klaatu begins fooling with some sort of gadget—
it looked kind of like a Weed-Eater, as I recall—and a trigger-
happy soldier-boy promptly shoots him in the arm. It turns
out, of course, that the gadget was a gift for the President. No
death ray here; just a simple star-to-star communicator.

That was in 1951. On that Saturday afternoon in Connecticut some six years later, the folks in the flying saucers looked and acted a good deal less friendly. Far from the noble and rather sad good looks of Michael Rennie as Klaatu, the space people in *Earth vs. the Flying Saucers* looked like old and extremely evil living trees, with their gnarled, shriveled bodies and their snarling old men's faces.

Rather than bringing a communicator to the President like any new ambassador bringing a token of his country's esteem, the saucer people in *Earth vs. the Flying Saucers* bring death rays, destruction, and, ultimately, all-out war. All of this—most particularly the destruction of Washington, D.C.—was rendered with marvelous reality by the special effects work of Ray Harryhausen a fellow who used to go to the movies with a chum named Ray Bradbury [famous science fiction writer today] when he was a kid.

Klaatu comes to extend the hand of friendship and brotherhood. He offers the people of Earth membership in a kind of interstellar United Nations—always provided we can put our unfortunate habit of killing each other by the millions behind us. The saucerians of *Earth vs. the Flying Saucers* come only to conquer, the last armada of a dying planet, old and greedy, seeking not peace but plunder.

The Day the Earth Stood Still is one of a select handful— the real science fiction movies. The ancient saucerians of *Earth vs. the Flying Saucers* are emissaries of a much more common breed of film—the horror-show. No nonsense about "It was to be a gift for your President" here; these folks simply descend upon Hugh Marlowe's Project Skyhook at Cape Canaveral and begin kicking ass.

It is in the space between these two philosophies that the terror was seeded, I think. If there is a line of force between such neatly opposing ideas, then the terror almost certainly grew there.

Because, just as the saucers were mounting their attack on Our Nation's Capital in the movie's final reel, everything just stopped. The screen went black. The theater was full of kids, but there was remarkably little disturbance. If you think back to the Saturday matinees of your misspent youth, you may recall that a bunch of kids at the movies has any number of ways of expressing its pique at the interruption of the film or its overdue commencement—rhythmic clapping; that great childhood tribal chant of "We-want-the-*show!* We-want-the-*show!* We-want-the-*show!*"; candy boxes that fly at the screen; popcorn boxes that become bugles. If some kid has had a Black Cat firecracker in his pocket since the last Fourth of July, he will take this opportunity to remove it, pass it around to his friends for their approval and admiration, and then light it and toss it over the balcony.

None of these things happened on that October day. The film hadn't broken; the projector had simply been turned off. And then the houselights began to come up, a totally unheard-of occurrence. We sat there looking around, blinking in the light like moles.

The manager walked out into the middle of the stage and held his hands up—quite unnecessarily—for quiet. Six years later, in 1963, I flashed on that moment when, one Friday afternoon in November, the guy who drove us home from school told us that the President [John F. Kennedy] had been shot in Dallas.

HORROR WORKS ON TWO LEVELS

If there is any truth or worth to the danse macabre [dance of death], it is simply that novels, movies, TV and radio programs—even the comic books—dealing with horror always do their work on two levels.

On top is the "gross-out" level—when Regan vomits in the priest's face or masturbates with a crucifix in *The Exorcist*, or when the raw-looking, terribly inside-out monster in John Frankenheimer's *Prophecy* crunches off the helicopter pilot's head like a Tootsie-Pop. The gross-out can be done with varying degrees of artistic finesse, but it's always there.

But on another, more potent level, the work of horror really is a dance—a moving, rhythmic search. And what it's looking for is the place where you, the viewer or the reader, live at your most primitive level. The work of horror is not interested in the civilized furniture of our lives. Such a work dances through these rooms which we have fitted out one piece at a time, each piece expressing—we hope!—our socially acceptable and pleasantly enlightened character. It is in search of another place, a room which may sometimes resemble the secret den of a Victorian gentleman, sometimes the torture chamber of the Spanish Inquisition . . . but perhaps most frequently and most successfully, the simple and brutally plain hole of a Stone Age cave-dweller.

Is horror art? On this second level, the work of horror can be nothing else; it achieves the level of art simply because it is looking for something beyond art, something that predates art: it is looking for what I would call phobic pressure points. The good horror tale will dance its way to the center of your life and find the secret door to the room you believed no one but you knew of—as both [novelist] Albert Camus and [songwriter] Billy Joel have pointed out, The Stranger makes us nervous . . . but we love to try on his face in secret.

Do spiders give you the horrors? Fine. We'll have spiders, as in *Tarantula, The Incredible Shrinking Man,* and *Kingdom of the Spiders.* What about rats? In James Herbert's novel of the same name, you can feel them crawl all over you . . . and eat you alive. How about snakes? That shut-in feeling? Heights? Or . . . whatever there is.

THE POWER OF THE MODERN MEDIA

Because books and movies are mass media, the field of horror has often been able to do better than even these personal fears over the last thirty years. During that period (and to a lesser degree, in the seventy or so years preceding), the horror genre has often been able to find national phobic pressure points, and those books and films which have been the most successful almost always seem to play upon and express fears which exist across a wide spectrum of people. Such fears, which are often political, economic, and psychological rather than supernatural, give the best work of horror a pleasing allegorical feel—and it's the one sort of allegory that most filmmakers seem at home with. Maybe because they know that if the shit starts getting too thick, they can always bring the monster shambling out of the darkness again. . . .

FEAR AND OUTER SPACE

We sat there in our seats like dummies, staring at the manager. He looked nervous and sallow—or perhaps that was only the footlights. We sat wondering what sort of catastrophe could have caused him to stop the movie just as it was reaching that apotheosis of all Saturday matinee shows, "the good part." And the way his voice trembled when he spoke did not add to anyone's sense of well-being.

"I want to tell you," he said in that trembly voice, "that the Russians have put a space satellite into orbit around the earth. They call it . . . *Spootnik*."

This piece of intelligence was greeted by absolute, tomb-like silence. We just sat there, a theaterful of 1950s kids with crew cuts, whiffle cuts, ponytails, ducktails, crinolines, chinos, jeans with cuffs, Captain Midnight rings; kids who had just discovered Chuck Berry and Little Richard on New York's one black rhythm and blues station, which we could get at night, wavering in and out like a powerful jive language from a distant planet. We were the kids who grew up on Captain Video and Terry and the Pirates. We were the kids who had seen Combat Casey kick the teeth out of North Korean gooks without number in the comic books. We were the kids who saw Richard Carlson catch thousands of dirty Commie spies in *I Led Three Lives*. We were the kids who had ponied up a quarter apiece to watch Hugh Marlowe in *Earth vs. the Flying Saucers* and got this piece of upsetting news as a kind of nasty bonus.

I remember this very clearly: cutting through that awful dead silence came one shrill voice, whether that of a boy or a girl I do not know; a voice that was near tears but that was also full of a frightening anger: "Oh, go show the movie, you liar!"

The manager did not even look toward the place from which that voice had come, and that was somehow the worst thing of all. Somehow that proved it. The Russians had beaten us into space. Somewhere over our heads, beeping triumphantly, was an electronic ball which had been launched and constructed behind the Iron Curtain [the Soviet Union and Eastern Europe]. Neither Captain Midnight nor Richard Carlson (who also starred in *Riders to the Stars;* and oh boy, the bitter irony in that) had been able to stop it. It was up there . . . and they called it Spootnik. The manager stood there for a moment longer, looking out at us as if he wished he had something else to say but could not think what it might be. Then he walked off and pretty soon the movie started up again.

COLD WAR PARANOIA AND THE NEW HORROR

So here's a question. You remember where you were when President Kennedy was assassinated. You remember where you were when you heard that RFK [Robert Fitzgerald Kennedy] had taken a dive in some hotel kitchen as the result of another crazy. Maybe you even remember where you were during the Cuban missile crisis.

Do you remember where you were when the Russians launched Sputnik I?

Terror—what [counterculture writer] Hunter Thompson calls "fear and loathing"—often arises from a pervasive sense of disestablishment; that things are in the unmaking. If that sense of unmaking is sudden and seems personal—if it hits you around the heart—then it lodges in the memory as a complete set. Just the fact that almost everyone remembers where he/she was at the instant he/she heard the news of the Kennedy assassination is something I find almost as interesting as the fact that one nurd with a mail-order gun was able to change the entire course of world history in just fourteen seconds or so. That moment of knowledge and the three-day spasm of stunned grief which followed it is perhaps the closest any people in history has ever come to a total period of mass consciousness and mass empathy and—in retrospect—mass memory: two hundred million people in a living frieze. Love cannot achieve that sort of across-the-board hammer-strike of emotion, apparently. More's the pity.

I'm not suggesting that the news of Sputnik's launching had anywhere near the same sort of effect on the American psyche (although it was not without effect; see, for instance, Tom Wolfe's amusing narrative of events following the successful Russian launch in his superlative book about our space program, *The Right Stuff*), but I am guessing that a great many kids—the war babies, we were called—remember the event as well as I do.

THE MODERN PIONEER SPIRIT

We were fertile ground for the seeds of terror, we war babies; we had been raised in a strange circus atmosphere of paranoia, patriotism, and national *hubris.* We were told that we were the greatest nation on earth and that any Iron Curtain outlaw who tried to draw down on us in that great saloon of international politics would discover who the fastest gun in the West was (as in Pat Frank's illuminating novel of the period, *Alas, Babylon*), but we were also told exactly what to keep in our fallout shelters and how long we would have to stay in there after we won the war. We had more to eat than any nation in the history of the world, but there were traces of Strontium-90 in our milk from nuclear testing.

We were the children of the men and women who won what Duke [John] Wayne used to call "the big one," and when the dust cleared, America was on top. We had replaced England as the colossus that stood astride the world. When the folks got together again to make me and millions of kids like me, London had been bombed almost flat, the sun was setting every twelve hours or so on the British Empire, and Russia had been bled nearly white in its war against the Nazis; during the siege of Stalingrad, Russian soldiers had been reduced to dining on their dead comrades. But not a single bomb had fallen on New York, and America had the lightest casualty rate of any major power involved in the war.

Further, we had a great history to draw upon (all short histories are great histories), particularly in matters of invention and innovation. Every grade-school teacher produced the same two words for the delectation of his/her students; two magic words glittering and glowing like a beautiful neon sign; two words of almost incredible power and grace; and these two words were: PIONEER SPIRIT. I and my fellow kids grew up secure in this knowledge of America's PIONEER SPIRIT—a knowledge that could be summed up in a litany of names learned by rote in the classroom. Eli Whitney. Samuel Morse. Alexander Graham Bell. Henry Ford. Robert Goddard. Wilbur and Orville Wright. Robert Oppenheimer. These men, ladies and gentlemen, all had one great thing in common. They were all Americans simply bursting with PIONEER SPIRIT. We were and always had been, in that pungent American phrase, fustest and bestest with the mostest.

And what a world stretched ahead! It was all outlined in the stories of Robert A. Heinlein, Lester del Rey, Alfred Bester, Stanley Weinbaum, and dozens of others! These dreams came in the last of the science fiction pulp magazines, which were shrinking and dying by that October in 1957 . . . but science fiction itself had never been in better shape. Space would be more than conquered, these writers told us; it would . . . it would be . . . why, it would be PIONEERED! Silver needles piercing the void, followed by flaming rockets lowering huge ships onto alien worlds, followed by hardy colonies full of men and women (*American* men and women, need one add) with PIONEER SPIRIT bursting from every pore. Mars would become our backyard, the new gold rush (or possibly the new rhodium rush) might well be in the asteroid belt . . . and ultimately, of course, the stars themselves would be ours—a glorious future awaited with tourists snapping Kodak prints of the six moons of Procyon IV and a Chevrolet JetCar assembly line on Sirius III. Earth itself would be transformed into a utopia that you could see on the cover of any '50s issue of *Fantasy and Science Fiction*, *Amazing Stories*, *Galaxy*, or *Astounding Stories*.

A future filled with the PIONEER SPIRIT; even better, a future filled with the *AMERICAN* PIONEER SPIRIT. See, for example, the cover of the original Bantam paperback edition of Ray Bradbury's *Martian Chronicles*. In this artistic vision—a figment of the artist's imagination and not of Bradbury's; there is nothing so ethnocentric or downright silly in this classic melding of science fiction and fantasy—the landing space travelers look a great deal like gyrenes storming up the beach at Saipan or Tarawa. It's a rocket instead of an LST [landing ship, tank] in the background, true, but their jut-jawed, automatic-brandishing commander might have stepped right out of a John Wayne movie: "Come on, you suckers, do you want to live forever? Where's your PIONEER SPIRIT?"

AMERICANS' ILLUSIONS THREATENED

This was the cradle of elementary political theory and tecnological dreamwork in which I and a great many other war babies were rocked until that day in October, when the cradle was rudely upended and all of us fell out. For me, it was the end of the sweet dream . . . and the beginning of the nightmare.

The children grasped the implication of what the Russians had done as well and as quickly as anyone else—certainly as fast as the politicians who were falling all over themselves to cut the good lumber out of this nasty deadfall. The big bombers that had smashed Berlin and Hamburg in World War II were even then, in 1957, becoming obsolete. A new

and ominous abbreviation had come into the working vocabulary of terror: ICBM [Intercontinental Ballistic Missile]. The
ICBMs, we understood, were only the German V-rockets
grown up. They would carry enormous payloads of nuclear
death and destruction, and if the Russkies tried anything
funny, we would simply blow them right off the face of the
earth. Watch out, Moscow! Here comes a big, hot dose of the
PIONEER SPIRIT for you, you turkeys!

Except that somehow, incredibly, the Russians were looking pretty good in the old ICBM department themselves. After all, ICBMs were only big rockets, and the Commies certainly hadn't lofted Sputnik I into orbit with a potato masher.

And in that context, the movie began again in Stratford,
with the ominous, warbling voices of the saucerians echoing
everywhere: *"Look to your skies . . . a warning will come from
your skies . . . look to your skies . . ."*

Stephen King, College Student

Sanford Phippen

Stephen King's college years at the University of Maine, Orono (1966–1970), have perhaps garnered less attention than his earlier childhood period as one of two sons of a single mother struggling to ward off destitution, or even his postcollege, pre-*Carrie* days teaching high school English and trying to support his own young family. This may be due to the fact that King himself has frequently memorialized his early youth in striking portraits of childhood in his works *It*, "The Body," *Hearts in Atlantis*, and *Dreamcatcher*. Yet as the following selection by fellow University of Maine alumnus Sanford Phippen points out, King's four years as a college English major were profoundly formative in his development as both writer and citizen.

Like many college students of his generation, King was swept up in the radical politics, antiestablishment attitude, and rock 'n' roll fervor of the times. The campus radical may have mellowed somewhat with maturity, yet progressive social criticism threads throughout King's work. Phippen's article portrays King as a passionately dedicated and remarkably prolific author of poetry, a muckraking column, and horror fiction—the last of which several of his professors, as would many later critics, viewed as a frivolous use of his talents.

He is certainly the University of Maine's most famous graduate. (Can you name another who has made the cover of *Time*?) What F. Scott Fitzgerald is to Princeton, what Nathaniel Haw-

Sanford Phippen, "Stephen King: The Master of Modern Horror at Maine," *The Maine Campus*, Fall 1989. Copyright © 1989 by *The Maine Campus*. Reproduced by permission.

thorne is to Bowdoin, and what Thomas Wolfe is to Chapel Hill, Stephen King is to Maine.

People tend to fall in love with authors more than with engineering programs, forestry schools—maybe even athletic teams. Look at the people who come to the state because of [writers] E.B. White, Robert McClosky, even Helen and Scott Nearing. On a recent literary tour of the Bangor-Brewer area, Lou Galbath and I had to cut short part of a planned itinerary because so many of the librarians and teachers, mostly from Ohio, wanted to be sure they reached Stephen King's house to have their pictures taken before it got too dark.

Students are now enrolling at Maine because of King's influence. And in the creative writing department, where I taught for a year (1978–79), his presence is strongly felt. One of my former colleagues says, "I don't mind Stephen King, but I wished he lived in Arizona. So many students try to imitate him—and badly. They think writing like this is an *easy* way to make money."

The influence of King on the university seems natural enough. The fact is that UMaine is where Stephen King started to become STEPHEN KING. Orono is where he first began to publish his work, both in his regular columns for the *Maine Campus* and the college literary magazine, and in national magazines like *Cavalier.* Orono is where he impressed his professors as a good student and was encouraged by them in his writing. Orono is where he received an important forum and feedback for his early work. Orono is where he made lasting friendships. And Orono is where he met his wife, Tabitha Spruce ('71) from Old Town.

Of course, the era he attended the university was also an important factor in the development of Stephen King. It didn't hurt to be a writer-in-the-making on a college campus during one of the most turbulent times of the twentieth century. Steve was a student from 1966 to 1970, and while no race riots or antiwar demonstrations got wildly out of hand at Maine, there were demonstrations and protests, there was a Students for Democratic Society [SDS] group on campus, and there was a three-day unofficial moratorium after the Kent State University tragedy in the spring of 1970. And Maine, like other U.S. colleges at the time, was undergoing many changes, especially in the areas of students' rights and residential life.

KING AS CAMPUS COLUMNIST

King's popular column "King's Garbage Truck," which appeared in the *Maine Campus* from February 20, 1969, through May 21, 1970, reflects much of what was going on at the time. While mostly he reviewed movies, TV shows, and rock music (just as he still does in his work), he did call for a general student strike on April 24, 1969. And he wrote in one column about what it was like to be called dirty names and have eggs thrown at you during a relatively peaceful "End the War" protest march on campus in May 1969. He attacked such establishment organizations as the All-Maine Women, Senior Skulls, Sophomore Owls, and Eagles, calling them irrelevant and elitist. In reaction to such groups, he invented his own organization which he called the Nitty Gritty Up Tight Society for a Campus with More Cools, and he handed out "gritties" or awards to those people at Maine who, in his opinion, did cool things. His columns also attacked Pope Paul, and supported the California grape pickers' strike in October 1969. On the other hand, he wrote in support of police officers and against those at the time who called cops "pigs."

In a March 3, 1970, column, he suggests that the university would be a better place if it got rid of all required courses and abolished requirements for all branches of the school. In one of his final columns (April 1970), he writes about how he changed from being a conservative who voted for Nixon in 1968 to becoming what he termed a "scummy radical bastard." The radical image of Stephen King was featured in a photo by Frank Kadi ('69) on the cover of the January 15, 1969, *Campus*. King looked as wild as one of his evil characters, sporting long hair, a beard, a deranged look in his eyes, grinning a buck-toothed grin, and pointing a double-barreled shotgun at the reader. Underneath the picture, in "coming-of-Christ" headline print, is the exclamation: "STUDY, DAMMIT!!"

KING AND POETRY

In a May 1, 1969, column, King wrote about being part of the first "special seminar" created at the university during the fall semester of 1968. This was Contemporary Poetry, taught by Burt Hatlen ('65) and Jim Bishop ('61), two of King's favorite instructors, and to whom, along with fellow English professor Edward M. "Ted" Holmes ('54G), he dedicated *The Long Walk*, one of the four novels written under King's pseudonym, Richard Bachman.

According to Hatlen, the special seminar courses were created to allow faculty and students to plan classes outside the curriculum. And students needed to apply for admission. The Contemporary Poetry seminar was limited to twelve students and involved a "very intense discussion about poetics, how you write poetry, and so on." Hatlen says that Steve "wasn't very theoretical, but on the fringes." (Tabby King, who was then a sophomore, says she'll never forgive Hatlen for not letting her in.)

As a sophomore, King had taken Hatlen for Modern American Literature, and Hatlen feels that this course had a long-term influence on King, for it's where he came into contact with [John] Steinbeck and [Willaim] Faulkner (King now collects first editions of Faulkner).

Before the contemporary poetry seminar, Jim Bishop had King as a student in 1966 in freshman English and he remembers "Steve's big physical presence" and how King was "religious about writing." He also remembers that King always had a paperback in his pocket, and knew all these authors that nobody else ever heard of.

"Steve was a nice kid, a good student, but never had a lot of social confidence," Bishop says. "Even then, though, he saw himself as a famous writer and he thought he could make money at it. Steve was writing continuously, industriously, and diligently. He was amiable, resilient, and created his own world."

In his introduction to *Moth*, a student literary magazine published in 1970, Jim Bishop wrote about that extraordinary poetry seminar: "From that seminar, which supposedly terminated in January 1969, came a half dozen or so energetic and highly individual young poets who have been rapping in hallways, in coffee shops, in front of Stevens Hall, or wherever any two of them chance to meet, ever since, and that original group has grown this year to a dozen, sometimes as many as twenty, who meet every other Friday in an informal workshop to read their poetry, alternatively to read and reassemble one another, and hopefully to emerge with a better understanding of themselves, their world, and their work.". . .

Besides Stephen King, whose poems "The Dark Man," "Donovan's Brain," and "Silence" were included in *Moth*, there are Tabby Spruce with six poems; Michael Alpert ('72), a Bangor publisher, who has since collaborated with King on a fancy edition of *The Eyes of the Dragon;* three of King's best friends from college—Jim Smith ('72), Dave Lyon ('70), and Bruce Holsapple ('73)—Diane McPherson (who designed the *Moth* cover); and George MacLeod ('72), King's former roommate. The others who have work in *Moth* are Susan Lienhard ('71), Stephen Black ('70), Mike Gilleland ('72), Sherry Dresser, and Jean Stewart.

The poetry workshop met frequently at the Maine Christian Association House on College Avenue, among other places, throughout King's senior year. Jim Bishop was on leave from teaching that year and living at Pemaquid Point. But he still commuted to Orono for the meetings. Tom Bailey and Graham Adams of the English faculty presided, and it was Adams who allowed King to teach a course as a senior undergraduate. Adams served as the front person, because the university wouldn't allow a student to teach a course. But King was, in reality, the teacher, and the course, naturally enough, was called "Popular Literature in America."

KING REMINISCES ABOUT COLLEGE

King's own thoughts about the poetry workshops and creative writing courses at Maine were recorded in interviews with the University of Southern Maine's *Presumscot* in 1977, and with UM's *Ubris II* in 1984.

"I realized that what I had for those years I was involved with the writing seminar was a big blank," King told *Ubris II.* "There were about forty to fifty poems, and two of them I've still got around. So for me, there was this tremendously exciting experience and nothing came of it. It was like being on a long drunk. But, on the other hand, I wasn't typical. For a lot of people, good did come of it."

When asked if he learned the craft of writing in college courses, King replied: "No, no, but I don't think it was bad. The creative writing courses at the college level are very important, but I don't think they're necessary. It's a supportive experience. . . . The best thing about it was that the art of writing was taken seriously, and that's an awfully good thing."

COFFEEHOUSES AND COUNTRY SONGS

In 1969–70, students from the workshop were involved with much more than poetry. George MacLeod, for instance, was one of the leaders of the student strike. Members of the group would often meet at the coffee shop which was part of the old bookstore in the Memorial Union.

Diane McPherson, . . . who was a member of both the seminar and the workshop, shared tutorial writing sessions with King under Ted Holmes. "We wrote independently but then got together once a week and it was great fun, often hilarious. I was the ideal audience for Steve's wildly inventive fantasies. My thing then was to cut all the extraneous adverbs and adjectives. Steve was pretty pop. He was writing exciting stories, but with no control."

McPherson also remembers King singing. "There was this coffeehouse on campus—The Ram's Horn—and there would be these open sings, or open hoots. People brought their instruments, and Steve would always sing country and western songs about this terrible loser who never had any luck. I remember thinking at that time that Steve was singing about a version of himself that rang true."

King is also remembered hanging out at the back booth of the Bear's Den with fellow students Jim Tierney ('69) . . . and Steve Williams ('60). And he was known to frequent the old Shamrock Bar across from Pat's Pizza where he would join friends and members of the more radical campus groups for folk music and beer.

EARLY PUBLICATIONS

At the end of the tutorial time with Professor Holmes, Ted sent McPherson's and King's stories to his agent, and soon after, King had a story accepted by *Cavalier*. "He decided early what kind of writer he wanted to be, and he went and did it," McPherson says. "He used to say, 'I'm hoping to have my own career.' Now and then I think how funny it is that I went to college with Stephen King."

Everyone agrees that the first person to officially declare King a writer was Ted Holmes. As reported in the book *Stephen King: The Art of Darkness* by Douglas E. Winter, King, as a sophomore, showed Burt Hatlen the manuscript of a novel he had written his freshman year. Hatlen in turn handed the manuscript to Holmes, who, after reading it, said ecstatically, "I think we've got a writer."

"When Steve was a junior and senior," Holmes says, "we had a lot of conferences over his work. He was a natural storyteller, of course, and his craftsmanship was always pretty good."

One of King's stories, "Night Surf" . . . eventually became *The Stand*. Other stories completed at UMaine were "Here There Be Tygers," "Cain Rose Up," "The Blue Air Compressor," and "Heavy Metal."

For most of the decade of the sixties, Ted Holmes was the sole creative writing teacher at Maine. Winthrop C. Libby, then president of the university, remembers a talk he once had with Holmes about King's prospects as an important professional writer. "Ted was not especially complimentary on that point. He said, as I recall, that while Steve certainly had a knack for storytelling, he wished that Steve would write more than horror stories."

Today, Holmes says of King's career, "I'm very glad that he's so successful. I respect his craftsmanship, but I haven't read all his books."

WRITER, READER, RADICAL

For his part, Libby remembers King as "essentially a very gentle person who acted the part of being a very wild man." Libby said that he'd see King "hovering around in the background" of student affairs committee meetings (King was elected to the Student Senate by the largest vote ever cast up to that time). "I'd always stop and chat with him; and my wife and I went to his wedding in Old Town, which was rather strange, because the ceremony was at the Catholic church and the reception at the Methodist" (Steve was the Methodist, Tabitha the Catholic).

As a freshman, King lived at 203 Gannett Hall. But after that first year, he moved off campus. In his senior year he remembers living alone in a "scuzzy riverside cabin not far from the university."

In his junior year, King lived on North Maine Street in Orono in a house that has since burned down. One of his roommates was George MacLeod. . . . There were two apartments for ten people, and MacLeod remembers King had a "whole regiment" of open beer bottles around his bed. He also remembers the future novelist's avid reading habits.

"Steve read like his life depended on it," MacLeod says. "He was writing and reading all the time. Basically he was an insecure kid who hid in books."

MacLeod remembers that a lot of energy from the poetry workshop went into politics, but he says that while King would make a lot of noise and contribute to the chaos of the times, he was not an effective leader for causes.

"He's a loose cannon as far as politics go," MacLeod says. "He was a noisy radical opposed to Vietnam, and he did lead a group of students one night to President Libby's house. He was kind of an odd person: on one hand very private and yet public in a loud way."

Some of the political gains that resulted from what MacLeod terms a coalition of splinter groups from the SDS and other activist organizations were a program for independent study, and having a pass/fail option instead of grades for students. "Steve was a figurehead for some radical efforts," claims MacLeod, "but basically he was middle-of-the-road in most areas. However, he was always there with his pitchfork and torch when you needed him."

MacLeod, who was a member of both the poetry seminar and workshop groups with King, also offered some insights into the popular novelist's personality. "Steve is uncomfortable with certain people and with large groups," he says. "He's erratic because he's nervous. He's a figurehead with feet of clay, and essentially he hasn't changed."

Emily Woodcock Templeton ('70), who audited the poetry workshop class that Steve was in, has some clear memories of the late sixties at Maine. "You felt like you were part of a school that was on the vanguard of great change, a time of building," she says. "People were working hard. Reading was something everyone was doing then. In contrast to today's atmosphere, a lot of people were at college to just read and learn. It shouldn't be forgotten that at Maine no one was looking down on the soldiers fighting in Vietnam, but we were against the war. The University of Maine was the only university in the U.S. at the time that held a blood drive for the soldiers. As for Steve King, he was one of the more committed people on campus, not a rabble-rouser, but he spoke out about what be thought."

David Bright ('70) was the editor of the *Maine Campus* when King began his "Garbage Truck" columns in 1969. He remembers King coming to him and saying he'd like to write a column. "Steve named it 'Garbage Truck' because you never know what you're going to find in a garbage truck."

Bright was amazed at how King would stroll in just before deadline, put the paper in the typewriter, crank out his column, and hand it to the editor. It would be "letter-perfect copy," Bright remembers, that would fit the space to the inch. "This is a guy who has at least seven stories going on in his head at the same time," Bright says.

THE WRITER BLOSSOMS

Even after he graduated from Maine, in the summer of 1970, when there was a summer *Maine Campus* edited by Bob Haskell, King wrote a regular column for the paper. This was called "Slade," the story of a western gunfighter. This column was the seed for King's novel *The Dark Tower*.

In the Afterword to *The Dark Tower* [I], King writes about how the conception for the story began to take shape in March of 1970. "During that spring semester, a sort of hush fell over my previously busy creative life—not a writer's block, but a sense that it was time to stop goofing around with a pick and shovel and get behind the controls of one big great God almighty steamshovel, a sense that it was time to try and dig something big out of the sand, even if the effort turned out to be an abysmal failure."

This statement indicates that King developed confidence in himself and his talent at quite an early age. David Bright attributes some of that development to the University of Maine.

"The University of Maine is a good place," Bright says.

"You can be just about anything you want to be here." He added that he thought the times, the atmosphere, and the type of campus that Win Libby created all contributed to the development of Stephen King.

"The university served King well," Bright wrote in an article in the *Portland Monthly*, "taking a rather shy but brilliant Maine boy and turning him into an outgoing, productive asset to the state, yet leaving intact his wit, character, and eye for observing the people around him."

Bright claims that Steve would like to provide more opportunity for other potential writers to do what he did at the university. "King sees a need for a program to help new writers develop," Bright says. "He envisions some sort of a foundation-supported artists' guild, which would help writers reave their families to Maine, pay their expenses, and find an environment in which to write."

Bright agrees with King that the university could do more for young writers. "The university did for King what it's supposed to do for its citizens," he says. "But the university has got to remember that some kids aren't as motivated as Steve King was."

A few years ago [in the 1980s], King did want to endow a creative writing chair in the English department, but there were some disagreements over how the gift was to be used and the matter fell through.

KING RECALLED BY HIS TEACHERS

King's former teachers at Maine disagree somewhat on his stature as a writer, but all seem to think highly of him as both a student and a person.

Robert Hunting was chairman of the English department and had King as a student in an English drama course. "Steve and I are good friends but I don't really read much of him," Hunting says. "I've read a couple of his books, but I like him better as a person than a writer. He's a very successful pop cult figure, and I'm a square. I have to remind myself though that Mozart also was a pop cult figure. Some of them become classics and some are forgotten.

"Steve was in my class as a senior," Hunting continued. "I was brand new here then. He was a very good student and helped me with the class. And I read his column with interest. Actually I got to know him better when he was coming back after graduation. He was always very generous with his time. He talked to the students in many classes. Then for one year, he was my colleague."

Hunting is referring to 1978, when King taught creative writing at Maine. Ulrich Wicks, the man who hired him, remembers King as a popular and effective teacher.

"Steve was very much liked and very good with students," agrees Hunting. He had all of these creative types. He was true and candid with them, but very kind also. I remember his saying to some very noisy young fellow that he'd have more of a chance with editors if he'd pay more attention to the nuts and bolts. He said they'd like it better if he'd spell better and if he'd write grammatical sentences. The student left happy."

Hunting says he has always been fond of Steve as a person and in later years as a public-spirited citizen. "I like the positions he takes, even if I'm not his most admiring reader. I don't think he'd mind me saying that, for I do admire him in so many ways."

ARTIST OR STORYTELLER?

One of the students Steve had in 1978 in his creative writing course was novelist Margaret Dickson, who admits she didn't even know who he was. She says he was a good teacher because he was interested in all of his students, and cared about them. "I found Steve a very generous, widely read, and interesting teacher," she says.

King helped start Dickson on her way as a novelist, as he had done with Michael Kimball and Rick Hautala.

Although Robert Hunting has not read many of King's

books, other veterans of the English department do keep up with their most famous student's works.

"I enjoy reading Steve," says Ulrich Wicks, "but he's a troubled person. There's a great deal in him that needs to come out. The unevenness of his work is a reflection of Steve's many selves."

Burt Hatlen thinks King is one of the most serious writers working today. And creative writing teacher Connie Hunting brushes off the criticism that King's works are shallow. "They're always saying that Steve doesn't say anything," she says, "but *The Stand* says something."

Professor Carroll Terrell says he quit the Maine Literary Association a couple of years ago over King. "I stopped going there because they had such awful opinions of him," he says. "And these opinions were based on not having read anything of his at all."

There does seem to be a group of people who refuse to read King—probably the same folks who make a big thing out of not watching TV or not listening to popular music.

Christopher Spruce, King's brother-in-law and the former manager of King's WZON radio station in Bangor, says this argument over whether King is an artist or just a good, entertaining storyteller is never-ending. "I can tell you that people should read his work seriously, because I believe he is a serious writer. He's not just out for a fast buck—why should he be at this point? There's a deep investment in his being the best writer he can be."

Connie Hunting says that although Stephen King has great influence on current writing students, they often pick up his tricks but not his deeper philosophical stances. "A novel like *The Stand* is not just a collection of horror—it's saying something very clearly. But the students only pick up on the exaggerated style and write stuff like 'the road regurgitated in front of us.' What they get is only the glitz."

Talking about her own friendship with Stephen King, Connie Hunting says, "People have very warm feelings about

Steve—it's not just that he's the world's best-selling novelist. It's because he's Steve and we know him, okay? It's not that we've got a stake in him. He's the neighborhood. He's the Maine neighborhood."

It is clear that King's four years at the University of Maine were a time of tremendous growth. No, UM didn't make Stephen King into the world's best-selling author—it didn't create that horrific and prolific imagination. But it did give him a solid foundation in literature and it did provide him with an environment where writing—most especially his own writing—was taken seriously. And more important, it gave him the freedom to explore, to be accepted for who he was, and to "act the part of a wild man," as Winthrop Libby said.

By his own account, as well as that of friends and faculty members, Stephen King left Maine with self-confidence and craftsmanship. Not a bad accomplishment for any college graduate.

King's Views on the Writing Process

Stephen King

Stephen King's 2000 nonfiction book *On Writing* blends observations on his craft with often humorous anecdotes and autobiographical candor. He is frank about his past struggles with alcohol and drugs and his more recent 1999 near-fatal accident, when he was struck by an out-of-control van whose driver was distracted by his dog. But the heart of the book is a passionate yet commonsensical view of the creative writing process. Unlike many artists, King avoids mystifying writing as an incomprehensible, divinely inspired process; rather, he speaks of the nuts and bolts of writing, from plot and character development to the importance of finding an optimal physical place in which to write.

In the following selection from *On Writing*, King begins, characteristically, by addressing a constant thorn in his side: the snobbery of serious literary critics regarding commercially successful writers. He next argues that to be a writer, one must read a lot. Even reading bad prose can be instructive, demonstrating to fledgling writers faults to avoid while cultivating an appreciation of truly first-rate fiction. Moreover, reading, unlike writing, is infinitely portable and can be done anywhere as long, he cautions, as it is done nowhere in the vicinity of a television.

There are no bad dogs, according to the title of a popular training manual, but don't tell that to the parent of a child mauled by a pit bull or a rottweiler; he or she is apt to bust your beak for you. And no matter how much I want to encourage the man or woman trying for the first time to write

Stephen King, *On Writing*. New York: Scribner, 2000. Copyright © 2000 by Stephen King. Reproduced by permission.

seriously, I can't lie and say there are no bad writers. Sorry, but there are *lots* of bad writers. Some are on-staff at your local newspaper, usually reviewing little-theater productions or pontificating about the local sports teams. Some have scribbled their way to homes in the Caribbean, leaving a trail of pulsing adverbs, wooden characters, and vile passive-voice constructions behind them. Others hold forth at open-mike poetry slams, wearing black turtlenecks and wrinkled khaki pants; they spout doggerel about "my angry lesbian breasts" and "the tilted alley where I cried my mother's name."

Writers form themselves into the pyramid we see in all areas of human talent and human creativity. At the bottom are the bad ones. Above them is a group which is slightly smaller but still large and welcoming; these are the competent writers. They may also be found on the staff of your local newspaper, on the racks at your local bookstore, and at poetry readings on Open Mike Night. These are folks who somehow understand that although a lesbian may be angry, her breasts will remain breasts.

The next level is much smaller. These are the really good writers. Above them—above almost all of us—are the Shakespeares, the Faulkners, the Yeatses, Shaws, and Eudora Weltys. They are geniuses, divine accidents, gifted in a way which is beyond our ability to understand, let alone attain. Shit, most geniuses aren't able to understand themselves, and many of them lead miserable lives, realizing (at least on some level) that they are nothing but fortunate freaks, the intellectual version of runway models who just happen to be born with the right cheekbones and with breasts which fit the image of an age.

COMPETENCE VS. TALENT

I am approaching the heart of this book with two theses, both simple. The first is that good writing consists of mastering the fundamentals (vocabulary, grammar, the elements of style) and then filling the third level of your toolbox with the right instruments. The second is that while it is impossible to make a competent writer out of a bad writer, and while it is equally impossible to make a great writer out of a good one, it *is* possible, with lots of hard work, dedication, and timely help, to make a good writer out of a merely competent one.

I'm afraid this idea is rejected by lots of critics and plenty of writing teachers, as well. Many of these are liberals in their politics but crustaceans in their chosen fields. Men and women who would take to the streets to protest the exclusion of African-Americans or Native Americans (I can imagine what Mr. Strunk [coauthor of the *Strunk and White* style manual] would have made of these politically correct but clunky terms) from the local country club are often the same men and women who tell their classes that writing ability is fixed and immutable; once a hack, always a hack. Even if a writer rises in the estimation of an influential critic or two, he/she always carries his/her early reputation along, like a respectable married woman who was a wild child as a teenager. Some people never forget, that's all, and a good deal of literary criticism serves only to reinforce a caste system which is as old as the intellectual snobbery which nurtured it. Raymond Chandler may be recognized now as an important figure in twentieth-century American literature, an early voice describing the anomie of urban life in the years after World War II, but there are plenty of critics who will reject such a judgment out of hand. He's a hack! they cry indignantly. A hack with pretensions! The worst kind! The kind who thinks he can pass for one of *us!*

Critics who try to rise above this intellectual hardening of the arteries usually meet with limited success. Their colleagues may accept Chandler into the company of the great, but are apt to seat him at the foot of the table. And there are always those whispers: *Came out of the pulp tradition, you know . . . carries himself well for one of those, doesn't he? . . . did you know he wrote for* Black Mask *in the thirties . . . yes, regrettable . . .*

Even Charles Dickens, the Shakespeare of the novel, has faced a constant critical attack as a result of his often sensational subject matter, his cheerful fecundity (when he wasn't creating novels, he and his wife were creating children), and, of course, his success with the book-reading groundlings of his time and ours. Critics and scholars have always been suspicious of popular success. Often their suspicions are justified. In other cases, these suspicions are used as an excuse not to think. No one can be as intellectually slothful as a really smart person; give smart people half a chance and they will ship their oars and drift . . . dozing to Byzantium, you might say.

Hard Work and Muses

So yes—I expect to be accused by some of promoting a brainless and happy Horatio Alger philosophy, defending my own less-than-spotless reputation while I'm at it, and of encouraging people who are "just not our sort, old chap" to apply for membership at the country club. I guess I can live with that. But before we go on, let me repeat my basic premise: if you're a bad writer, no one can help you become a good one, or even a competent one. If you're good and want to be great . . . fuhgeddaboudit.

What follows is everything I know about how to write good fiction. I'll be as brief as possible, because your time is valuable and so is mine, and we both understand that the hours we spend talking about writing is time we don't spend actually *doing* it. I'll be as encouraging as possible, because it's my nature and because I love this job. I want you to love it, too. But if you don't want to work your ass off, you have no business trying to write well—settle back into competency and be grateful you have even that much to fall back on. There is a muse,* but he's not going to come fluttering down into your writing room and scatter creative fairy-dust

---

* Traditionally, the muses were women, but mine's a guy; I'm afraid we'll just have to live with that.

all over your typewriter or computer station. He lives in the ground. He's a basement guy. You have to descend to his level, and once you get down there you have to furnish an apartment for him to live in. You have to do all the grunt labor, in other words, while the muse sits and smokes cigars and admires his bowling trophies and pretends to ignore you. Do you think this is fair? *I* think it's fair. He may not be much to look at, that muse-guy, and he may not be much of a conversationalist (what I get out of mine is mostly surly grunts, unless he's on duty), but he's got the inspiration. It's right that you should do all the work and burn all the midnight oil, because the guy with the cigar and the little wings has got a bag of magic. There's stuff in there that can change your life.

Believe me, I know.

READING AS PLEASURE AND PROCESS

If you want to be a writer, you must do two things above all others: read a lot and write a lot. There's no way around these two things that I'm aware of, no shortcut.

I'm a slow reader, but I usually get through seventy or eighty books a year, mostly fiction. I don't read in order to study the craft; I read because I like to read. It's what I do at night, kicked back in my blue chair. Similarly, I don't read fiction to study the art of fiction, but simply because I like stories. Yet there is a learning process going on. Every book you pick up has its own lesson or lessons, and quite often the bad books have more to teach than the good ones.

When I was in the eighth grade, I happened upon a paperback novel by Murray Leinster, a science fiction pulp writer who did most of his work during the forties and fifties, when magazines like *Amazing Stories* paid a penny a word. I had read other books by Mr. Leinster, enough to know that the quality of his writing was uneven. This particular tale, which was about mining in the asteroid belt, was one of his less successful efforts. Only that's too kind. It was terrible, actually, a story populated by paper-thin characters and driven by outlandish plot developments. Worst of all (or so it seemed to me at the time), Leinster had fallen in love with the word *zestful.* Characters watched the approach of ore-bearing asteroids with *zestful smiles.* Characters sat down to supper aboard their mining ship with *zestful anticipation.* Near the end of the book, the hero swept the large-breasted, blonde heroine into a *zestful embrace.* For me, it was the literary equivalent of a smallpox vaccination: I have never, so far as I know, used the word *zestful* in a novel or a story. God willing, I never will.

Asteroid Miners (which wasn't the title, but that's close enough) was an important book in my life as a reader. Almost everyone can remember losing his or her virginity, and most writers can remember the first book he/she put down thinking: *I can do better than this. Hell, I* am *doing better than this!* What could be more encouraging to the struggling writer than to realize his/her work is unquestionably better than that of someone who actually got paid for his/her stuff?

LEARNING FROM GOOD AND BAD WRITING

One learns most clearly what not to do by reading bad prose—one novel like *Asteroid Miners* (or *Valley of the Dolls, Flowers in the Attic,* and *The Bridges of Madison County,* to name just a few) is worth a semester at a good writing school, even with the superstar guest lecturers thrown in.

Good writing, on the other hand, teaches the learning writer about style, graceful narration, plot development, the creation of believable characters, and truth-telling. A novel like *The Grapes of Wrath* may fill a new writer with feelings of despair and good old-fashioned jealousy—"I'll never be able to write anything that good, not if I live to be a thousand"—but such feelings can also serve as a spur, goading the writer to work harder and aim higher. Being swept away by a combination of great story and great writing—of being flattened, in fact—is part of every writer's necessary formation. You cannot hope to sweep someone else away by the force of your writing until it has been done to you.

So we read to experience the mediocre and the outright rotten; such experience helps us to recognize those things when they begin to creep into our own work, and to steer clear of them. We also read in order to measure ourselves against the good and the great, to get a sense of all that can be done. And we read in order to experience different styles.

You may find yourself adopting a style you find particularly exciting, and there's nothing wrong with that. When I read Ray Bradbury as a kid, I wrote like Ray Bradbury—everything green and wondrous and seen through a lens smeared with the grease of nostalgia. When I read James M. Cain, everything I wrote came out clipped and stripped and hard-boiled. When I read [H.P.] Lovecraft, my prose became luxurious and Byzantine. I wrote stories in my teenage years where all these styles merged, creating a kind of hilarious stew. This sort of stylistic blending is a necessary part of developing one's own style, but it doesn't occur in a vacuum. You have to read widely, constantly refining (and redefining) your own work as you do so. It's hard for me to believe that people who read very little (or not at all in some cases) should presume to write and expect people to like what they have written, but I know it's true. If I had a nickel for every person who ever told me he/she wanted to become a writer but "didn't have time to read," I could buy myself a pretty good steak dinner. Can I be blunt on this subject? If you don't have time to read, you don't have the time (or the tools) to write. Simple as that.

HOW TO READ EVERYWHERE

Reading is the creative center of a writer's life. I take a book with me everywhere I go, and find there are all sorts of opportunities to dip in. The trick is to teach yourself to read in small sips as well as in long swallows. Waiting rooms were made for books—of course! But so are theater lobbies before the show, long and boring checkout lines, and everyone's favorite, the john. You can even read while you're driving, thanks to the audiobook revolution. Of the books I read each year, anywhere from six to a dozen are on tape. As for all the wonderful radio you will be missing, come on—how many times can you listen to Deep Purple sing "Highway Star"?

Reading at meals is considered rude in polite society, but if you expect to succeed as a writer, rudeness should be the second-to-least of your concerns. The least of all should be polite society and what it expects. If you intend to write as truthfully as you can, your days as a member of polite society are numbered, anyway.

Where else can you read? There's always the treadmill, or whatever you use down at the local health club to get aerobic. I try to spend an hour doing that every day, and I think I'd go mad without a good novel to keep me company. Most exercise facilities (at home as well as outside it) are now equipped with TVs, but TV—while working out or anywhere else—really is about the last thing an aspiring writer needs. If you feel you must have the news analyst blowhards on CNN while you exercise, or the stock market blowhards on MSNBC, or the sports blowhards on ESPN, it's time for you to question how serious you really are about becoming a writer. You must be prepared to do some serious turning inward toward the life of the imagination, and that means, I'm afraid, that Geraldo, Keith Obermann, and Jay Leno must go. Reading takes time, and the glass teat takes too much of it.

Once weaned from the ephemeral craving for TV, most people will find they enjoy the time they spend reading. I'd like to suggest that turning off that endlessly quacking box is apt to improve the quality of your life as well as the quality of your writing. And how much of a sacrifice are we talking about here? How many *Frasier* and *ER* reruns does it take to make one American life complete? How many Richard Simmons infomercials? How many whiteboy/fatboy Beltway insiders on

CNN? Oh man, don't get me started. Jerry-Springer-Dr.-Dre-Judge-Judy-Jerry-Falwell-Donny-and-Marie, I rest my case.

THE LIMITS OF "REHEARSAL"

When my son Owen was seven or so, he fell in love with Bruce Springsteen's E Street Band, particularly with Clarence Clemons, the band's burly sax player. Owen decided he wanted to learn to play like Clarence. My wife and I were amused and delighted by this ambition. We were also hopeful, as any parent would be, that our kid would turn out to be talented, perhaps even some sort of prodigy. We got Owen a tenor saxophone for Christmas and lessons with Gordon Bowie, one of the local music men. Then we crossed our fingers and hoped for the best.

Seven months later I suggested to my wife that it was time to discontinue the sax lessons, if Owen concurred. Owen did, and with palpable relief—he hadn't wanted to say it himself, especially not after asking for the sax in the first place, but seven months had been long enough for him to realize that, while he might love Clarence Clemons's big sound, the saxophone was simply not for him—God had not given him that particular talent.

I knew, not because Owen stopped practicing, but because he was practicing only during the periods Mr. Bowie had set for him: half an hour after school four days a week, plus an hour on the weekends. Owen mastered the scales and the notes—nothing wrong with his memory, his lungs, or his eye-hand coordination—but we never heard him taking off, surprising himself with something new, blissing himself out. And as soon as his practice time was over, it was back into the case with the horn, and there it stayed until the next lesson or practice-time. What this suggested to me was that when it came to the sax and my son, there was never going to be any real play-time; it was all going to be rehearsal. That's no good. If there's no joy in it, it's just no good. It's best to go on to some other area, where the deposits of talent may be richer and the fun quotient higher.

Talent renders the whole idea of rehearsal meaningless; when you find something at which you are talented, you do it (whatever *it* is) until your fingers bleed or your eyes are ready to fall out of your head. Even when no one is listening (or reading, or watching), every outing is a bravura performance, because you as the creator are happy. Perhaps even ecstatic. That goes for reading and writing as well as for playing a musical instrument, hitting a baseball, or running the four-forty. The sort of strenuous reading and writing program I advocate—four to six hours a day, every day—will not seem strenuous if you really enjoy doing these things and have an aptitude for them; in fact, you may be following such a program already. If you feel you need permission to do all the reading and writing your little heart desires, however, consider it hereby granted by yours truly.

The real importance of reading is that it creates an ease and intimacy with the process of writing; one comes to the country of the writer with one's papers and identification pretty much in order. Constant reading will pull you into a place (a mind-set, if you like the phrase) where you can write eagerly and without self-consciousness. It also offers you a constantly growing knowledge of what has been done and what hasn't, what is trite and what is fresh, what works and what just lies there dying (or dead) on the page. The more you read, the less apt you are to make a fool of yourself with your pen or word processor.

Is Stephen King Calling It Quits?

Chris Nashawaty

In a 2002 interview, Stephen King spoke with *Entertainment Weekly* writer Chris Nashawaty for a cover story that provided both an overview of his career and the writer's stunning revelation that he intends to cease publishing fiction. King implies that injuries from his near-fatal 1999 accident, which still cause him pain, play a part in his apparent decision to write only for himself, despite the fact that he is finally garnering the long-elusive respect of the literary establishment. It is, of course, as yet impossible to judge whether King will follow through on his pledge to forgo publishing his work. What is clear from the *Entertainment Weekly* story, however, is that King's dark humor, candor, and lack of pretension remain intact as he approaches a career crossroads.

Stephen King limps toward his car like an innocent man being led to the electric chair and slides behind the wheel of his black Mercedes convertible—grimacing in pain as he pulls his right leg into the driver's side like a piece of deadwood. It still hurts like hell three years after his accident. The van that slammed into him on a rural Maine road on June 19, 1999, not only shattered his right leg to powder but broke his hip and four ribs, chipped his spine in eight places, and collapsed one of his lungs. He should be dead. In fact, he and his wife have a nickname for his postaccident life: "The Bonus Round." All things considered, though, he says he feels fine. And frankly, he's bored hearing himself talk about it. Just like

Chris Nashawaty "Stephen King Calls It Quits," *Entertainment Weekly*, September 27, 2002, pp. 20–28. Copyright © 2002 by Entertainment Weekly, Inc. Reproduced by permission.

he's bored hearing himself talk about a lot of things, including his shocking decision to call it quits and stop publishing. "I've killed enough of the world's trees" is all he'll say at first.

King comes right out and says that he doesn't want to do this interview at all, hence his death-row demeanor. Nothing personal. You seem like a nice enough fella. But even so, he'd just rather not. It makes him uncomfortable. He says that everyone already knows what little there is to know about him. And that the folks who come up to Maine to talk to him pretty much know what they're going to print before they get there anyway—that beneath his folksy Yankee demeanor he's some sort of twisted, ghoulish freak. Why else would he write what he does?

Still, there's no turning back now. He knows that his new supernatural-car novel *From a Buick 8* is coming out and, well, he wouldn't mind seeing it rack up Tom Clancy numbers. And since his publisher, Scribner, asked real nicely, he just sort of caved. But if he absolutely has to go through with this, he might as well do it with a bacon cheeseburger in his belly. So King revs the engine, ignores the blinking seat-belt indicator, and peels off onto the mean streets of Bangor, following the scent of deep-fried food.

THE "REGULAR GUY"

At Nicky's, a '50s-style diner that looks like the inspiration for *Pulp Fiction*'s Jack Rabbit Slim's minus all the Hollywood razzle-dazzle, King is greeted like a regular. It's the kind of place where even if "Wipe Out" weren't playing on the jukebox, it should be. On the way to his table, King tries to settle a longstanding bet about his beloved Boston Red Sox with one of the joint's employees. And as he takes his seat, he immediately orders a plate of batter-dipped mushrooms and sour cream to hold him over till the bacon-topped burger comes—pretty much thumbing his nose, and his ticker, at the whole notion of "The Bonus Round."

After we order, I pull out a copy of King's high school

yearbook photo and slide it across the table. The student staring out from the picture is all hornrimmed nerdiness. His NASA buzz cut gives his sizable ears nowhere to hide. His square suit and tie make him look like he might knock at your door to tell you about The Good News. But he seems to sport the sly grin of a guy who knows deep down he's going to make it out of this damn place.

The 55-year-old King smiles at the teenager looking back at him and says that actually, no, he didn't think he'd get out at all. "The thing about that guy in the picture is, you say, 'Would he ever in his wildest dreams have imagined *this* happening?' And the answer is no. But if you said to him, 'Are you afraid of that?' he would have said '*F—, no!*' I wasn't afraid of anything." King picks up the picture and takes a deeper look, squinting at his younger self. "Doesn't it sort of look like a picture of a guy who'd end up as an accountant, or dead in Vietnam, or possibly a mass murderer?"

As he polishes off his burger, licking stray bits of mustard from his fingers, the waitress comes over. King shoots her a smile and says, "I want a piece of strawberry cheesecake." Then he looks across the table at me and says, "You do too, you just don't know it."

FROM POVERTY TO WEALTH

In his 2000 memoir *On Writing*, Stephen King says that his earliest memory is being 2½ or 3 and, pretending he was the Ringling Bros.' circus strongboy, hoisting a cement cinder block that unfortunately housed a wasps' nest—a scene that was later borrowed and put to use in *The Shining*. He doesn't remember what happened a year earlier, when his father, Donald, walked out to get a pack of smokes and never returned. For years afterward, King, his older brother, David, and his mother all referred to the missing man in their life as "Daddy Done," as in "Daddy Done Left."

There was a period during his childhood when King's mother, Ruth, who died 29 years ago, left him in the revolving-door care of relatives. He guessed it was because she had a breakdown. Recently, though, he found out the real reason: that his AWOL father had run up debts all over the Northeast and she was off working to make good on them. "I remember before we went off to grammar school, she got all serious and took us aside and said, 'People are going to ask what your father does. Tell them he's in the Navy.' She didn't want anybody to know that he left her."

Maybe it's because King is so wealthy now that he can detail his early poverty with such humor and candor. The man who's sold hundreds of millions of books and had more movies adapted from his work than any other American author laughs about working at a woolen mill where rats the size of Chevy pickups would prowl the graveyard shift; how he toiled at a laundry like his mother, dreading that he was repeating her life; and how he and his college sweetheart-turned-wife, Tabitha, lived in a trailer in Maine with two kids—Naomi and Joe, with Owen yet to come—by the time he was 24, subsisting on donated food. He even finds a sort of gallows humor in the $6,400 a year he made as a schoolteacher. "When I left I was about to be put in charge of the debate club, and that would have been the final straw. I could see myself 20 years later with an ulcer, a rampant drinking habit, divorced, paying alimony, and miserable because I wasn't doing what I was supposed to be doing."

EARLY STORIES

What he was supposed to be doing, of course, was writing. King says that he's known this all along—ever since he was a kid cranking out morose short stories about ledge jumpers for a neighborhood newsletter. So at night, after teaching, or after sweating through a shift at the laundry, he would sit in the trailer he and his wife called home, and write for as long as he could. It wasn't long before King's stories found an audience. Granted, it was through such low-rent "gentlemen's magazines" as *Cavalier*, but he could crank out those stories in a few hours and make up to 500 bucks a pop. Now, King cracks up recalling some of his early literary benefactors. "*Dude Gent, Juggs, Adam, Swank, Gallery,* you name it." And he laughs recalling how his wife would photocopy the articles for King's mother—careful to black out the X-rated ads that surrounded his stories. "They were all for stag films and jellies to increase your potency that you slather on your tool. All that stuff," he says. King even tried his hand at penning pornographic stories because he heard they paid well. "I tried, but I just collapsed laughing. I couldn't do it. I got as far as twins having sex in a birdbath."

THE BREAKTHROUGH

In the early '70s, King started his first novel, *Carrie.* At first he didn't know where it was going, so he tossed it into the trash. His wife fished it out, read it, and encouraged him to continue. King now regards *Carrie's* success as the high point of his career. He was 25 and still teaching school when he sold the novel to Doubleday. His advance was a mere $2,500, which he quickly spent to replace the old Buick beater whose transmission was threatening to drop out. He and his wife also moved out of the trailer. But it was selling the book's paperback rights that finally gave King the financial freedom to chuck all the crappy jobs once and for all. "I thought we'd get between $25,000 and $60,000. And when they told me that it was $400,000, I knew I could take the next few years to write full-time—which, to me, sounded like heaven."

From that moment, King wrote like a man possessed. In the 10 years beginning with *Carrie's* publication in 1974, King published 20 books, including *Salem's Lot, The Stand,* and *Pet Sematary.* And with a mix of pride and bashfulness, he now admits to pounding out *The Running Man,* one of several books he released under the pseudonym Richard Bachman, in 10 days. But King's output was more than just the work of a man possessed by writing. He'd also developed a serious addiction to both cocaine and booze—what he now terms "the honey traps" of success.

KING BATTLES DRUGS AND ALCOHOL

King says he was so messed up that he doesn't even remember rewriting 1981's *Cujo*. He can still look at the scribbled revisions on the manuscript, but has no clue who put them there. He scoffs at the phrase *leisure drugs* because, he says, "with me, getting high was never leisurely." For example, with cocaine, he says, "the idea was that you were going to get it and you were going to write three books in a week! If I'd known how instantly I'd become hooked I never would have touched it. It's like running into a noose." Because King was so far away from his editor and publisher in New York, no one knew how severe the problem was, or how, for example, King would stay up all night furiously typing with cotton swabs stuffed up his nose to stanch the bleeding. But his longtime editor Chuck Verrill recalls the first time he witnessed the train wreck with his own eyes. King was in New York doing postproduction on a movie he'd directed called *Maximum Overdrive* when Verrill met him about the manuscript of *It*. "He was gargling Listerine and popping pills. He was still a nice guy and coherent, but he did seem to be strung out."

Finally, in 1987, Tabby called together her husband's friends and family for an intervention—dumping a trash bag full of beer cans, gram bottles of coke, Valium, Xanax, and bottles of Robitussin and NyQuil onto the floor with a shape-up-or-ship-out ultimatum. Still, it would take King another year to clean up. "I didn't have an experience with a white light or anything like that. I was on the turnpike out here one day. I remember right where I was. I was between exit 46 and exit 47. Cloudy day. Just driving along doing my business, thinking about getting high. And I thought to myself, You don't have to do this anymore if you don't want to. It's like it wasn't my voice."

KING TAKES ON THE CRITICS

Stephen King gets a bad rap, and don't think it doesn't piss him off. He hates how highbrow critics write him off as some sort of bogeyman hack—a guilty pleasure whose page-turners go down like a fistful of honey-roasted peanuts. He knows the suspicion the literary establishment has about authors who bang out as many books as he does. And the snobbery that comes with selling so many copies of them. He knows all of this and simmers at the hypocrisy of it.

About *On Writing*—a large portion of which is dedicated to advice for fledgling writers, including a section on habits to avoid—King has joked that the idea of him authoring a book about how to write is "like the town whore trying to teach women how to behave." It's a good line. But you get the sense that he doesn't believe it for a second—and that he also likes playing the outsider. That even if he were invited to rub leather-patched elbows and clink highballs with John Updike and Tom Wolfe, he wouldn't want to.

Still, he wouldn't mind a little more respect. "I remember I got a review on *The Stand*," he says. "I'd worked on this book for two or three years on and off. Busted my hump. And it turns up as this two-line squib saying '*Rosemary's Baby* goes to the Devil. Avoid it.' And I thought to myself I hate this! First of all, the guy didn't read the book—I can tell by what he's saying. And second of all, I hate the elitist, snotty attitude of it. And it says something that I can remember that review word for word 22 years later."

RESPECT AT LAST

In 1990, King published his first story for *The New Yorker*—a long way from the pages of *Juggs*—and it's around that time that something curious started to happen. The jury on him seemed to go back into their chambers and amend their verdict. "Yeah, it's made a difference at how I'm looked at," says King. "I don't get bookended with Dean Koontz quite as often."

The story was called "Head Down," and it was about his son's Little League team. Since then, several of his other *New Yorker* stories have been reprinted in the collection *Everything's Eventual.* But even though King's pleased with his late-career nod from the belles lettres set (he won warm reviews for a "literary" novel, 1998's *Bag of Bones*), he still seems suspicious. In fact, King guesses that the reason he won the O. Henry Award in 1996 for his short story "The Man in the Black Suit" was because the submissions didn't have the authors' names attached. "There's an immediate attitude that anyone who's reaching a large, popular audience—what they're doing is crap! Because the popular mind is crap! I mean, you've got these two places," he says, spreading his hands apart. "Here is 'high literature,' and then you've got 'popular fiction' over here. And in between is this great big river of misunderstanding. There are a lot of people, I feel, who are dedicated to keeping the clubhouse white."

Adds his editor Verrill: "I think a lot of people in the literary community look at horror as a gutter genre. So I don't think he's really embraced as a member of whatever pantheon there is. I mean, you don't think of Philip Roth and Stephen King in the same sentence. But I think the door has been finally opened to him."

In other words, it's a strange time to be giving it all up.

TIME TO RETIRE?

After lunch, as the surf-guitar crescendo of "Wipe Out" kicks in for the third time in an hour, King pops a toothpick into his mouth and limps toward the parking lot. That's when he finally wears down and talks about his decision to retire.

King's been coy about hanging it up in the past. After his accident, he joked that he didn't want to become a parody of himself, or a punchline like Harold Robbins. But this time, King insists, he's serious. And he seems to have his game plan mapped out. First, his new novel about a troop of Pennsylvania state policemen and their relationship with a possessed vintage car, *From a Buick 8*, will come out. After that, he says he's got the final three installments of his projected seven-volume fantasy series *The Dark Tower*—the saga of a lone gunslinger named Roland, which he began 33 years ago. Then after that, no more Stephen King books. "People are going to say a year and a half from now that the talk of re-tirement was ridiculous because those will come out, but af-ter that. . ."

No more books?

"Sure. Yeah. First of all, I'd never stop writing because I don't know what I'd do between nine and one every day. But I'd stop publishing. I don't need the money."

Just file them in the drawer?

"Why not? What's wrong with that? J.D. Salinger's been doing it for years! There's a story I heard about this lady who works in a bank in New Hampshire, where Salinger has a safety deposit box. And every year he'd go in with a wrapped box. And if you've ever worked in publishing, you know what an 8-by-10 box is—it's a manuscript. So she said, 'Are those books you're putting away?' And he said yes. And she said, 'Are you ever going to publish them?' And he looked down his nose at her and said, 'What for?' And it's one of those sto-ries where you gotta say, 'If it ain't true, it oughta be.'"

King gets so animated telling this story, he heads the wrong way down a one-way street and rattles off an impres-sively ornate string of profanities. I ask him, what about his fans, and he gets visibly upset.

"I've always rejected the idea that every book had to be available to every consumer. I used to get these angry letters about the *Dark Tower* books when they were just limited edi-tions. Somebody would say, 'Well, I want that book!' And I'm like, 'Hey, there are people in hell who want ice water, too!'"

Actually, it seems like everyone but Stephen King thinks he won't stop. "I've been involved with Steve since 1997," says his publisher at Scribner, Susan Moldow, "and in that time I would say there's been six different stories about how

Stephen King is going to stop writing. So I, for a variety of reasons, obviously, desire to take those threats with a grain of salt." Adds Peter Straub, who's coauthored *The Talisman* and *Black House* with King: "I have a great deal of difficulty believing it. . . . It might be his last novel for the *year*."

Still, as King says, the *Dark Tower* books may be the most fitting place to end. When it's all said and done, the gunslinger saga will weigh in at nearly 5,000 pages. It's like King's *Remembrance of Things Past*, only with a much higher body count. "This finishes it," he insists. "It's the sequel to everything. And in a sense, once these books are done, there's nothing else to say."

Added to that, King says, is the fact that his new novel, *From a Buick 8*, is "as close as I want to get to repeating myself—it's not *Christine*, but it's a novel about a car. . . . I mean, experience tells us that every writer gets to a point where he starts to lose his power. And you have to ask yourself this: How much is enough? Yeah, I might have some more books I can write, but honest to God, I've published damn near 50 books now. That's a lot more than Norman Mailer's ever gonna publish, I guarantee you."

But won't he miss it? The rush of seeing one of his novels released?

"Absolutely not. Would I miss that? What? I mean, I'm going to Detroit this time and sign books at a Wal-Mart. What a thrill! Are you kidding?"

THE BURDEN OF FAME

King parks his car in front of a low-rise building in an industrial park near the Bangor airport where he tends to the administrative business of Stephen King, Inc. In his office, King hobbles over to an old record player and throws on a bawdy old rock song by Freddy "Boom Boom" Cannon called "Buzz Buzz A-Diddle-It." In the corner, there's a gigantic stack of galleys sent by publishers hopeful that King will find the time to blurb them. Not far away is King's house, where he does all of his writing and where a steady stream of tour buses idles in front of his driveway. King hates that—and everything else that comes along with the first part of "famous writer."

Like the author in *Misery*, King admits that his relationship with his fans is sometimes overwhelming. And, naturally, because of the kinds of stories he writes, some of King's fans can border on Annie Wilkes–like [Annie Wilkes is the main character in *Misery*] devotion. "It's like, did you ever see the movie *The Day of the Locust?*" he asks. "That scene where they tear this guy apart? It's the American freak show: Tom Cruise, Bruce Springsteen, Stephen King, John Grisham, Bob Dylan—we're all freaks. That's what we are. And people come to look at us."

Of course, there's one name he left off that list. Another author whose fans trek to backwater New England to gawk at: J.D. Salinger. And perhaps he doesn't realize yet, but by calling it quits, Stephen King may only fuel the thing he wants to escape. In fact, it's so horrifically ironic that it seems like the perfect idea for his next book . . . should he ever decide to write one.

CHAPTER 2

Overarching Themes and Conventions in King's Fiction

READINGS ON
STEPHEN KING

King and the Heritage of Horror

Garyn G. Roberts

The following selection by Garyn G. Roberts discusses some of King's most significant influences in the "dark fantasy" genre, including Edgar Allan Poe, Ray Bradbury, H.P. Lovecraft, Shirley Jackson, and J.R.R. Tolkien. Yet while examining King's literary heritage, Roberts also points out that King is not a mere "borrower" from the writers who influenced him; he is also an inventor who has reimagined and reinvigorated the standard trappings of horror fiction (including vampires, werewolves, and other "uncanny" phenomena). These transformations are further reflected in the many movie versions of King's works. Roberts also praises King's vernacular prose style, which has frequently been a target of derision for critics of literary fiction. To those who denigrate King's avoidance of intricately metaphoric language and "thick description," Roberts suggests that the very everydayness of King's narrative style marks his stories as both universal and, despite the supernatural content, oddly realistic.

Garyn G. Roberts, who is a professor of English and communications at Northwest Michigan College, is also the author of *Dick Tracy and American Culture: Morality and Mythology, Text and Context* (1993) and the *Prentice Hall Anthology of Science Fiction and Fantasy* (2000).

[Since the early 1970s,] Stephen King has not only revolutionized the world of popular literature, he has taught us—onlookers, consumers, and critics alike—a thing or two about

Garyn G. Roberts, "Of Mad Dogs and Firestarters—The Incomparable Stephen King," *The Gothic World of Stephen King: Landscape of Nightmares*, edited by Gary Hoppenstand and Ray B. Browne. Bowling Green, OH: Bowling Green State University Popular Press, 1987. Copyright © 1987 by Bowling Green State University Popular Press. Reproduced by permission of the University of Wisconsin Press.

ourselves as individuals, and as members of a larger world culture. For King himself is a product of his individual experiences and cultural inheritances, and he mirrors what we are all about.

To date, not the most prolific of wordsmiths, King is the most commercially successful author of all time. Each new King novel or short story collection becomes a multi-million copy seller, and is destined to rise to the top of the *New York Times* Bestseller List in a few short weeks. "In little more than ten years, some fifty million copies of his books have been sold worldwide and thirteen motion pictures have been based on his work," stated Douglas Winter in 1985. And frightening, in more ways than one, is that Stephen King is only forty-years-old (b. September 21, 1947) and has a literary career ahead of him that boggles the mind. His "art of darkness" has just begun.

But, how original is the Dark Fantasy of Stephen King? John G. Cawelti suggests in his *Adventure, Mystery and Romance* (1976) that popular stories are a carefully crafted balance of convention and invention, or extended from that idea—fact and fantasy, the old and the new. It follows then that there is a degree of newness and freshness in King's tales of the macabre. And, there is an element of the old. . . . No, the very old—the ancient. Precisely what are the conventions and inventions of this contemporary grandmaster's electric prose?

KING'S HERITAGE OF HORROR

Stephen King came about as a "brand name" largely because the culture in which he emerged created, produced, and nurtured him. The tales that have been burned into the typewritten page and word processor computer disk, and ultimately bestselling novel, at the hands of King stem from a heritage of horror. In the mid–nineteenth century, there was Edgar Allan Poe; in the early twentieth—Howard Phillips Lovecraft; and in the waning years of the twentieth—

Stephen King. And, there were, are and will be others before, in between and after. King did not just come around; he's been centuries in the making. The definitive survey and study of the Horror genre in the mass media—King's own *Danse Macabre* (1979)—is not just a wonderfully insightful and profound study of Dark Fantasy, it is King's own dissection of his heritage of horror. Douglas Winter, the number one biographer of King with the obvious exception of King himself, has produced further works that substantiate the notion of King as an outgrowth of a heritage of horror. These are, most notably, *Stephen King: The Art of Darkness* (1984), and his (Winter's) interview with King published in *Faces of Fear* (1985).

About his early writing King notes, "I would have short stories where I started off sounding like Ray Bradbury and ended up sounding like Clark Ashton Smith—or even worse, they would start off as James M. Cain and end up as H.P. Lovecraft." King was, and is, an avid student of those who preceded him in his field. Particularly in the case of the 1930s "Weird Tales" published in the pulp magazine with the same name (the golden age for this the most important publication of dark fantasy and weird fiction), King finds fodder for his literary soul. In the fifties, that period in which the master found himself in his impressionable childhood, the science fiction/horror movies of the day like *The Thing* (1951) and *The Creature From the Black Lagoon* (1954) had particular impacts on his future writing, as did the emergence of the new American art form called "Rock 'N' Roll." The fifties and sixties also showcased Richard Matheson's and Rod Serling's teleplays for *The Twilight Zone* for the aspiring author. These people and events, and more, became the foundation for the house of King.

OLD TRADITIONS, MODERN THEMES

Both the novels and short stories of the Stephen King canon evidence a number of old traditions and time-tested themes which have manifested themselves in modern forms. Ray Bradbury's *Dark Carnival* (1947) (later cut to about two thirds its original length in *The October Country* (1955)) provided, and provides, a harvest of dark fantasy and weird fiction which has long been imitated and emulated in the work of King. Emerging from Bradbury's Dark Carnival mythos was the novel *Something Wicked This Way Comes* (1962), and there were his novels *Fahrenheit 451* (1953) (where firemen burned books!) and *The Martian Chronicles* (1950) (perhaps the "Best" piece of science fiction ever done). There were also those wonderfully twisted tales of the macabre collected in books of the always underrated, but consistently excellent Robert Bloch, and later, 1959's *Psycho* by Bloch (from which, of course, [director] Alfred Hitchcock and [actor] Tony Perkins have reaped a rather macabre immortality). In addition to Bradbury, to a degree, King's work evidences remnants of the work of H.P. Lovecraft, Robert E. Howard (King's "Gunslinger" stories are straight out of the Heroic Fantasy of Howard) and Clark Ashton Smith—the three musketeers of *Weird Tales*. And, there were others. King notes, "In college, I would go around with a John D. MacDonald book, or a collection of short stories by Robert Bloch, and some asshole would say, 'Why are you reading that?' and I'd say, 'Hey, this man is a great writer.'" But, he adds, "The guy who taught me to do what I am doing is Richard Matheson. . . ." Richard Matheson . . . along with Robert Bloch, Ray Bradbury and Fredric Brown—the most underrated American author of the twentieth century. While Matheson is most often remembered for his contributions to *The Twilight Zone* television program, where he, Rod Serling, and Charles Beaumont were the primary creative forces, Matheson also produced the landmark novels *I Am Legend.* (1954) and *The Incredible Shrinking Man* (1956)—an existential trek into oblivion where death is the welcomed end.

The heritage of horror that produced and embraced all the aforementioned people and events goes back even further. In fact, like many popular culture forms, stories of horror and the supernatural can be traced back to folklore, and even further, the earliest recorded beginnings of man. For it is death and after-life, and stories of the same, which have been man's most basic concern since the dawn of time. In folklore, two particular motifs in such stories have been prevalent. These are "The Hook Story" and "Tales of the Tarot." In fact, King himself addresses these influences in *Danse Macabre.* From the latter, the earliest examples of stories of vampires, werewolves, and nameless abominations appeared. King has retold all three of these "tales of the tarot" in his work.

KING'S MONSTERS AND VAMPIRES

Yet, where specifically are Bradbury and company reincarnated in the King canon? King's first bestseller, *Carrie,* appeared in 1974. Douglas Winter notes, "*Carrie* is largely about how women find their own channels of power, and what men fear about women and women's sexuality. . . ." Along with Brian De Palma's movie adaptation of the novel, *Carrie* launched King's popularity. The novel, and movie, are essentially a portrayal of the physical and psychological horrors of adolescence. Carrie, herself, however, does not experience the "normal" metamorphosis so often equated with this awkward human transformation. She is abused by her mother and classmates—home and society—alike, the same affliction that haunted Frankenstein's monster, various and assorted vampires (vampyres)—Dracula included, and the werewolf (wehr-wolf).

Speaking of vampires, in *'Salem's Lot* (1975), King recreates the classic vampire story, focusing on a town full of vampires rather than one isolated member of the living dead. Here, he also throws in the terrors of the haunted house, which, as in Edgar Allan Poe's "The Fall of the House of Usher," represent the horrors and inner workings of individual and collective minds alike. The Marsten house in *'Salem's Lot* is a great house that serves as a central symbol of the town in which it rests, and further, the individual and social mind alike. The haunted house motif in Stephen King's work only begins here. This motif is enhanced and is the basis for King's first hardcover bestseller—*The Shining* (1977). In this story, the Overlook Hotel is that house. Haunted houses have been the forte of gothic stories for centuries, as in Horace Walpole's *The Castle of Otranto* (1764), and Poe's nineteenth century tale of the house of Usher. In contemporary literature, before the work of King there were also Richard Matheson's *Hell House* in 1971 (which King acknowledges as a major influence on *The Shining*) and Shirley Jackson's *The Haunting of Hill House* (1959), and so on. The reason however, that the haunted house story, and the horror story in general works, and King mentions this in several places, is that the reading audience feels an empathy for and affinity with the person or people caught in the house. In *The Shining*, we feel an affinity with young Danny Torrance who is trapped in the structure which has driven his family to madness.

MASTERPIECES OF EPIC HORROR

Maybe the height of Stephen King's literary career to date came with the appearance of *The Shining* and the novel which followed shortly thereafter—*The Stand* (1978). *The Stand* turned out to be a leading contender for the title of best Stephen King novel. Douglas Winter explains the events that led to *The Stand* . . .

> He [King] was haunted by a news story that he had read about an accidental chemical/biological warfare spill in Utah that had nearly endangered Salt Lake City; it reminded him of George R. Stewart's science fiction novel *Earth Abides* (1949), in which a plague decimates the world. One day, while listening to a gospel radio station, he heard a preacher repeat the phrase "Once in every generation a plague will fall among them." King liked the sound of the phrase so much that he tacked it above his typewriter. . . .

Winter deems *The Stand* an epic fantasy much in the realm

of Tolkien and E.R. Eddison. *The Dead Zone* (1979), a political horror novel, followed, and again the central idea, in
this case political horror and intrigue, was a time tested storyline. Dino De Laurentiis' production values, Christopher
Walken's performance in the starring role of English teacher
Johnny Smith, and Martin Sheen's portrayal of the megalo-
maniacal politician Greg Stillson in the movie of the same
name, made this, without doubt, the best film adaptation of
a King novel to date.

Ray Bradbury turned out *Fahrenheit 451* in 1953 and
King produced *Firestarter* in 1980. More than similar story-
lines tied these two works together. Both were released in
limited edition asbestos covers, as well as mass market edi-
tions. "In 'The Mist'" (a King novella originally appearing in
Kirby McCauley's edited horror collection *Dark Forces* and
. . . reprinted in *Skeleton Crew*), Stephen King conjures the
quintessential faceless horror: a white opaque mist that en-
shrouds the northeastern United States (if not the world) as
the apparent result of an accident at a secret government fa-
cility," claims Douglas Winter. This, of course, is reminiscent
of King's own work in *The Stand*. Years before *The Stand*,
however, faceless horrors similar to the "white opaque mist"
in "The Mist" scourged the earth's population in popular fiction. William Hope Hodgson (1887–1918), accomplished
World War I hero for England, built several of his Sargasso
Sea stories and other such fantasies around this notion of a
faceless mist, fog, or wind. Ray Bradbury's "The Wind" (a
classic 1943 Weird Tale) is a perfect example of this.

> It's a big cloud of vapors, winds from all over the world
> . . . I know its feeding grounds, I know where it is born
> and where parts of it expire. For that reason, it hates me,
> and my books that tell how to defeat it. It doesn't want
> me preaching anymore. It wants to incorporate me into
> its huge body to give it knowledge. It wants me on its
> own side!

John Carpenter directed the motion picture *The Fog* in 1980 and Dennis Etchison wrote the novelization for the same, and the list of other precedents for "The Mist" goes on and on.

WEREWOLVES AND OTHER BEASTS

Two of King's dark fantasies, *Cujo* (1981) and *Cycle of the Werewolf* (1983), are retellings of the classic werewolf story. Both breathe new life (or death?) into this very old storyline. The title character of *Cujo* is a mad dog. There is not the exact form of transformation of human to beast that is characteristic of the old werewolf story. But, *Cujo* certainly is derivative of that archetypal storyline in other ways. As the title of *Cycle of the Werewolf* suggests, the focus of this King work (which is indeed a treasure when coupled with the magnificent illustrations of Berni Wrightson) is a dissection and discussion of the transformation process the human/werewolf entity experiences according to ancient folklore.

Pet Sematary (1984) is in some ways King's most horrifying tale because the terror extends beyond mere human death as we know it; it deals with the mysteries of the afterlife. George Romero and John Russo, director and writer of *The Night of the Living Dead* movies and books which have endeared themselves to more than a cult following in the sixties, seventies, and eighties, are surely an influence on *Pet Sematary*. Again, other precedents for King's work exist. His novel *It!* (1986) is an affectionate tribute to all the monsters that have haunted the movie screen, mass market novel and other popular media for decades.

THE ART OF THE VERNACULAR

The heritage of horror from which Dark Fantasy's contemporary grandmaster draws is perhaps self evident. And, King is the first to acknowledge all those creators, writers, monsters, media that have fed his literary soul. Yet, it would be only part of the larger picture if we claimed that this heritage of horror is the sole explanation for King's success (in our hearts as well as in publishers' bank accounts). There is indeed an inventional aspect to the works—no, master-pieces—of King. Essentially, these inventions come in two forms. First, there is King's successful updating of old themes, and his ability to recontextualize the "horrors" of the Horror story for a contemporary audience. King has poured his life experiences, as an individual and as a member of a larger culture, into his stories. And, as a regular, decent guy, he recounts adventures we can all relate to. We haven't personally seen a werewolf or a vampire, but King's conception of these are the same as ours. We know that when we meet that werewolf or vampire, it will be exactly as King has described them. Second, there is King's dexterity with the English language that few, if any, can match. While he claims to have no identifiable, conscious style, King has made the vernacular equal "Art." He told Douglas Winter, "I always wrote for myself, and then I looked for a market that was somewhere in the ballpark of what I was doing." That ballpark was, and is, the American, and now world, public.

The Art of Balance in King's Novels

Edwin F. Casebeer

One near-universal assumption about commercial fiction is that, unlike its "literary" counterpart, its narrative provides tidy closure: Villains are punished; heroes are rewarded; and loose plot threads are neatly tied up by the story's final page. Popular audiences, it is argued, want pure escapism and "happily ever after" endings. Yet these narrative conventions are consistently defied throughout the fiction of Stephen King. Innocent children die along with sympathetic adult characters; good deeds go unrewarded; and occasionally, evil triumphs. King's world, however, is not a pessimistic one as much as an *ambivalent* one, as Edwin F. Casebeer argues in the following selection. Good and evil coexist, sometimes in a single character and often in the novel's central conflict. Casebeer argues that King's realism and ability to depict opposing realities preclude his being pigeonholed as a mere horror writer.

Before his retirement, Edwin F. Casebeer was a professor of English at Indiana University. He has published widely on Stephen King, Peter Straub, and Herman Hesse.

Stephen King is the most popular horror novelist today (and also the most popular novelist). He is the only writer ever to have made the Forbes 500 [list of wealthiest Americans]; his annual income exceeds that of some third-world countries. His works are a significant percentage of the book industry's annual inventory. The average American recognizes his name and face. Yet, paradoxically, his novels also top the lists of cen-

Edwin F. Casebeer, "Stephen King's Canon: The Art of Balance," *A Dark Night's Dreaming: Contemporary American Horror Fiction*, edited by Tony Magistrale and Michael A. Morrison. Columbia: University of South Carolina Press, 1996. Copyright © 1996 by the University of South Carolina. Reproduced by permission.

sored authors. Perhaps that is because he creates fiction and cinema about that which we would rather avoid: modern meaninglessness, physical corruptibility, and death. Do the fictional situations he presents argue for a decline in our culture's energy for life, a descending depression and despair that lends enchantment to the graveyard, the kind of apocalyptic view that often ends centuries and heralds new human hells? Or is his appeal understandable in a way that affirms our culture and its willingness to deal with its dilemmas?

If we begin with Stephen King's status among his immediate peers—the horror novelists—the reasons for his broad appeal are clear. He has taken command of the field by writing representative masterworks: the vampire novel *('Salem's Lot)*, the monster novel *(The Dark Half)*, wild talent fiction *(Carrie)*, zombie fiction *(Pet Sematary)*, diabolic possession fiction *(Christine)*, and realistic horror fiction *(Misery)*. His presence in the field extends to its very boundaries.

KING AND GENRE FICTION

But King is actually a genre novelist; that is, he writes in all of the major popular genres now marketed to the country's largest reading population: horror, fantasy, science fiction, the western, the mystery, and the romance. While he works in pure forms *('Salem's Lot* as a vampire novel, *Cycle of the Werewolf* as a werewolf novel, *The Talisman* as a quest fantasy, and *The Running Man* as science fiction), he often mixes genres. An early example is *The Stand*, particularly its first published edition, which begins as one form of the science fiction novel (the apocalyptic), evolves into a second form (the utopian), and concludes as a fantasy which blends elements of the quest like [J.R.R.] Tolkien's *Lord of the Rings* trilogy with Christian apocalyptic fantasy like *The Omen* trilogy. Similarly, his *Dark Tower* trilogy combines apocalyptic science fiction with Arthurian quest fantasy, itself subordinated to the western, and then introduces science fiction's alternate worlds concept. The standard detective mystery does much to shape *The Dark Half, Needful Things*, and *Dolores Claiborne*, while the Gothic romance and the feminist novel are essential features of *Misery, Gerald's Game*, and *Dolores Claiborne*. The resulting breadth gives his fiction a much wider appeal than might come to a "pure" horror writer.

But King's appeal is even broader than that of a genre writer. From the beginning of his career, he was responsive to those horror writers of his decade, like Ira Levin, who moved from the traditional confines of the *fantastique* to establish analogies between the world that we all occupy and the horror novel's traditional settings, situations, plots, and characters. King, too, grounds fantasy in realism. In fact, his earliest published work, *Rage* (published under the Richard Bachman pseudonym), is a capable realistic novel. Motivated by his own boyhood and his involvement with his children, King's early novels demonstrate strong characterizations of preadolescent boys and small children. In the ensuing years, he has added to his palette, and now is taking up the challenge of realistic female protagonists.

EVERYDAY HORROR

King's appeal thus broadens even further: this realism opens up a subtext that addresses urgent contemporary concerns. From his youth, he has been a man of his generation; a man with deep political awareness and involvement. As has been elaborated critically by such works as Tony Magistrale's *Landscape of Fear* and Douglas Winter's *The Art of Darkness*, King has created many novels which allegorically address current social dilemmas: the corruption of school and church *(Rage, Carrie, Christine)*, the government *(The Long Walk, Firestarter, The Running Man, The Stand, The Dead Zone)*, the small town *('Salem's Lot, It, Needful Things, Tommyknockers)*, the family *(The Shining, Cujo, It, Christine)*, and heterosexual relationships *(Gerald's Game, Dolores Claiborne)*. Thus, King's work offers more than mere escape fiction or "adrenaline" fiction; it urges readers to confront squarely and disturbingly the horror in their own lives. The resulting depth connects him to an audience drawn to literature more "serious" than horror or genre fiction. His model has inspired enough followers to cause horror fiction to move to the front of bookstores and the top of the *New York Times'* bestseller list. It is not so much that the reading public has developed a perverse taste for horror as it is that, emulating King, horror writers have broadened and deepened their art enough to address us all on issues of consequence.

Paramount among these issues is death. As James Hillman pointed out in *Revisioning Psychology*, contemporary Western culture is the first extensive culture which has had to consider death as an ending, rather than as a transformation. Instead of believing in a transformation into an angel or devil, animal, or star, today's rationalists regard being as matter and unanimated being as refuse. Founded upon such materialism, the contemporary state and school have reinterpreted reality so as to provide for the here and now, and have maintained a polite skepticism about other realities. King repeatedly dramatizes, from an evolving perspective, the dilemma in which we find ourselves: we are without resources before the imminence of our own deaths and the catastrophe of the deaths of those we love. Adopting (such as in *Carrie*) a contemporary existentialist attitude (where the only constants are isolation, decay, and death), King explores such values (acts, creations, children) as may survive death or those entertained by other cultures (as in *The Stand*). In other novels (such as *The Talisman* and *The Dark Tower* series) King will entertain the possibilities suggested by post-Einsteinian physicists (the multiverse, the reality of process and the nonexistence of time, space, and matter). As in *It*, King looks at possibilities suggested by the psychoanalytic architects of reality, particularly the Jungian theory [psychoanalytic theory developed by Carl Jung] of an archetypal dimension underlying matter—a dimension that can be apprehended and molded by the artistic imagination. Although King sometimes ends his novels in nausea *(Pet Sematary)* or nothingness *(Carrie)*, normally he views the human condition in terms of possibilities and affirmations. Again representative of his generation—and his American community (small-town New England)—those affirmations are based upon what is possible for the individual, particularly the individual not blinded by rationalism. He displays deep distrust for any human configuration larger than the family.

THE ART OF BALANCE

Although King's thematic reach is wide and deep, ascertaining his position on any given issue is not simple. This ambiguity also underlies his broad appeal, for vastly different readers may arrive at vastly different conclusions about his agenda. King seems, in a novel like *The Stand*, to be able to appreciate the validity of the opposed positions of a small-town Christian, Republican American with a high school education and a sophisticated, liberal, and urban existentialist. In a way, like Shakespeare, he does not conclusively resolve a plot or commit irrevocably to the agenda of a specific character or group of characters involved in the conflict. But his noncommitment is so submerged that readers normally assume (as they have with Shakespeare for centuries) that he agrees with them; he economically gestures toward the possibility of gestalt, not a specific gestalt. On the contrary, his chief artistic talent—the talent that has kept all of his work in print throughout his career and is likely to keep it in print—is his ability to balance opposing realities. The reader must resolve the issues. If we supinely regard King as simply a popular artist and expect a canned resolution, we often will find his resolutions unsatisfying. If we invest the energy in tipping his balance toward ourselves, we will behold in the artistic experience an affirming and illuminating mirror of our problems and our solutions.

Such a mirror develops not only from King's choice of situations of great concern to us, but by his technique of characterization. Here again, he achieves balance, gains breadth and depth of appeal. In one sense, King is a highly accomplished realist with a keen eye for the nuances of image and voice; but, in another, his characters are archetypal with origins in myth and folktale. Characters fall into two large groups—the sketch and the multidimensional. One of his true talents is the sketch: he is able to populate novels like *'Salem's Lot*, *The Stand*, and *The Tommyknockers* with hundreds of briefly executed, vivid characters—each efficiently caught in a telling and representative moment that is often grotesque and generally memorable. King can make credible, as in *The Stand*, a plot that quite literally involves a whole country. He sketches characters from the South, New York, New England, the West, from the rural and urban blue-collar class, the middle class, the criminal and indigent, the police, the army, the entertainment world, and the clerks and functionaries of cities and small towns from all over America. These characters, placed in highly detailed topographies, create for us the realistic element of his fantasies so central in enabling us to accept their supernatural premises. As King said in an interview with Magistrale: "The work underlines again and again that I am not merely dealing with the surreal and the fantastic but, more important, using the surreal and the fantastic to examine the motivations of people and the society and the institutions they create."

CHARACTER DEVELOPMENT AND POINTS OF VIEW

King's realistic techniques for creating the primary multidimensional characters significantly differ from those producing the sketch. Generally speaking, he avoids the customary expository visual portrait of a primary character; he prefers to develop the character internally. Thus, by beginning in the character's sensorium, we can project more quickly and directly into it than we might if the objectification of a physical description was between us and it: existing as the bound Jessie Burlingame in *Gerald's Game*, we see, hear, touch, taste, and smell her experience of her world; and from these physical experiences we enter into and share her psychological presence. Generally, we find that psychological presence to be archetypal—the anima. Like any popular artist working with the stereotypical, King is always on the border of creating Jungian personae and plots emanating from the cultural unconscious. Therefore, however individually a multidimensional character may be textured, it feels very familiar as we settle into it.

But King goes a step further, particularly in his more epic novels, by exemplifying the theories of such neo-Jungian thinkers as Hillman: (1) the human psyche is basically a location for a cast of personae in dynamic relationship with one another; (2) the one-persona psyche—humanity's current and dominant commitment to unity, integration, and control—is pathological (the excesses of the rationalistic materialist); and (3) the universe and its inhabitants can only be seen clearly through multiple and dynamic perspectives. Thus, except in novellas and short stories, King generally prefers multiple points of view. Here he is influenced by modernists (such as Faulkner) and by cinema: perspective follows setting—and if the setting contains different characters, he still develops multiple points of view. In the larger novels, typically King pits a group of comrades against a common threat, a dynamic for which he found precedent in both Tolkien's *The Ring* trilogy and [Bram] Stoker's *Dracula*. Though the details produced by setting and sensorium conceal the fact, each comrade is a persona—a specialized and archetypal figure such as the child, the old man, the lover, the teacher, the healer, etc. As the plot progresses and each persona contributes its vision, the remaining personae subsume these perspectives and evolve into a single (hero or heroine) or dyadic (lovers or parent/child) protagonist with the capacity to defeat or stalemate the antagonist, which itself is often a persona embodying death, decay, or meaninglessness.

Just as often, however, the antagonist is the monstrous.

King has a particularly complex attitude toward such a persona. Like Clive Barker, King is able to see the positive side of the monstrous—its incredible energy and commitment, its individuality, and its ability to function in the unknown. Unlike Barker, he is not ready to embrace the monstrous and let it transform him. Again, balance prevails. In *Danse Macabre*, King analyzes the function of author and antagonist in novels. For him, the authorial is not the autobiographical; the "King" is another persona—the folksy, small-town Maine citizen of the commercials, of the prefaces, and of the authorial asides. The persona of the author agrees with the norms of the community. But the antagonist (as monster) is that shadow aspect of us which finds its reality in the individual, the bizarre, and the grotesque. This antagonist seeks to tyrannically control or to destroy rather than to belong, which is dynamic rather than centered and driven rather than ordered. We contain both and we come to the novel to experience both. Their conflict will never be settled, for it is the essence of what they are: opposites that define one another. Although Thad Beaumont, the protagonist of *The Dark Half*, wins his conflict with George Stark (the monster within him) we learn in *Needful Things* that he has lost his love, his art, and his family—he has settled back into alcoholism. In summary, the traditional horror novel, such as Bram Stoker's *Dracula*, excises or conquers the antagonist; the postmodernist horror novel, such as Clive Barker's works, transforms the protagonist into the antagonist, or vice versa; and King's novels balance these processes.

Tribe and Community

The end result of such a dynamic perception of character and structure is that the novel becomes psyche: that is, it is the location of archetypal personae and their dynamics. It is the interface between the psyches of writer and reader, a template of the soul, a mirror in which we see ourselves most clearly in terrain we least care to explore, the nightworld of death and monstrosity. Seen from the above perspectives, King becomes a modern shaman employing magic (the fantasy image, childhood imagination) to lead his culture into self-discovery where it most needs to look while maintaining commitment to love, family, and community—for King is also a husband, father, and highly visible "social" presence. Again he balances: he is of the tribe and he directs the tribe. No wonder we read him; no wonder we approach him with caution.

Because of his inclination to balance consecutive novels by opposing them to one another, these propositions apply more to the broad characteristics and processes of the canon rather than to individual novels. But his novels also fall into categories in which the same striving toward the balancing of opposing forces is evident: the community, the child, the writer, the woman, and the quest. These categories not only provide a more useful way of approaching King's fiction specifically than would a chronological or genre discussion, but they also focus the preceding theoretical discussion. Each category is a broad, shared foundation with the reader upon which and through which King can consistently design and redesign his social allegories and the psyche's archetypal templates that so consistently and profoundly link him with his audience.

King's writings about the community establish him as one of the country's major regionalist writers whose influences can be traced to the New England Gothic writers, Thornton Wilder's *Our Town*, and the novels of William Faulkner. The community which King most often chooses to present is one inspired by the town of his childhood—Durham, Maine. Sometimes the town is Jerusalem's Lot of the *'Salem's Lot* stories, Haven of *The Tommyknockers*, or Castle Rock—the setting of such works as "The Body," *Cujo*, *The Dead Zone*, *The Dark Half*, and *Needful Things*. A citizen of his region, King believes that the most politically viable unit is one small enough to hear and respond to individual opinion; as in *The Stand*, cities like New York regularly appear in an advanced state of disruption and the federal government responds only to the reality of its paper and its power.

Although community is more feasible in a small town than in a large city, in King's small towns it is rare. More frequently, their citizens (as in *'Salem's Lot*, *The Tommyknockers*, and *Needful Things*) are caught up in materialistic pursuits that lead them into conflict with their neighbors. This conflict results in a community held together by conformity rather than cooperation, with narcissism and the closed door, fealty to no code but self-gratification, and apocalypse simmering beneath the surface. Yet—to stress King's seeking of balance in this category—there appears the option of a better way of life. The Boulder Free Zone of *The Stand* comes closest to such a utopia: it is small, it accords a place to each according to need and talent, and it attends to the individual. But King is ambivalent about such a grassroots democracy; the true reason for the survival of the Free Zone is the emergence of an elite presiding coterie composed of exceptional individuals with exceptional social conscience. When events demand the sacrifice of most of these people and the Free Zone becomes too large for rule by their dialogue, Stu Redman and Fran Goldsmith (the surviving hero and heroine) conclude that their community now is simply recycling the former decadent and materialist world. They opt for a more viable social unit: the family. And they leave the Free Zone for the locale of King's own family, Maine.

FAMILY DYNAMICS IN KING'S FICTION

To understand King's strong focus on the family and the child requires recognition that during his career he has been a husband and father of two boys and a girl. During their childhood, he generally worked at home, but brought his family with him on the rare occasions when he left Maine. Thus, his family is often major material; he need only look up from the word processor to find grist. And as his own children have aged, so has the presence of the child diminished in his novels. The category of the child arises for a second reason: in his own development, King has had to reencounter himself as child and boy in order to remove the blocks to his becoming a man: "The idea is to go back and confront your childhood, in a sense relive it if you can, so that you can be whole." Also in this category are early novels such as *Rage* (begun while he was in high school), *The Long Walk*, and *Carrie* (written by a young man dealing with problems posed by family and organized adult society).

Among King's most endearing characters are small children such as Danny Torrance of *The Shining* and Charlie McGee of *Firestarter*. In their characterization, he avoids the potential sentimentality that often sinks such efforts by manipulating sentences that seamlessly weave together the diction and phrasing of both child and adult, thus conveying the being of the one and the perspective of the other. The second paragraph introducing Danny provides an example: "Now it was five o'clock, and although he didn't have a watch and couldn't tell time too well yet anyway, he was aware of passing time by the lengthening of the shadows, and by the golden cast that now tinged the afternoon light." The first subordinate clause is childishly run-on in structure and uses Danny's diction, while the second main clause is complex-compound within itself—its subordinate elements are parallel and its diction is the polysyllabic format typical of the narrator in King's lyric mode. Such a combination of styles and perspectives works so well because King adheres to the romantic belief that the child is the father of the man. It may be that children are superior in wisdom and psychological talents to adults simply because the latter are corrupted by psyches shrunken by materialism and rationalism—but they are superior. Thus, Danny is one with time and space, almost godlike in his perception of those dimensions in the haunted Hotel Overlook, while Charlie's power over the material world establishes her as an angel of apocalypse when she incinerates the Shop (King's version of the CIA).

King's adolescents can also be superior to his adults. In

fact, the major reason for grouping the adolescent with the child is that, normally, King's adolescents are prepubescent: they have no explicit sexual identity and are still more child than adult. It is in such adolescents that we see his attempt to achieve yet another kind of balance—between the two stages of life. While the child has intimations of immortality, the adult has knowledge of death. Thus, the Castle Rock novella "The Body" (made into the excellent film by Rob Reiner entitled *Stand By Me*) initiates its four boys by leading them not into a sexual encounter, but into another rite of passage: their first encounter with death as the corpse of a fifth boy. Similarly, in *It*, a group of boys encounters and prevails over the protean incarnation of every human's deepest fear; and in *The Talisman*, co-written with Peter Straub, a trio of boys (an archetypal id, ego, and superego) transcend the force of this reality to enter a reality in which death is unempowered. Sometimes, as in *Carrie*, *The Stand*, and *Christine*, death and sexuality are negatively related: as Carrie becomes sexual, she becomes monstrous and an angel of the apocalypse. The sexual foreplay of Nadine and Harold in *The Stand* is a clear symptom of their degenerate state. As Arnie becomes sexual, Christine corrupts him—even Arnie's benevolent alter ego, Dennis, discovers that his first love turns to ashes. In his most recent novels, King demonstrates a mature and central sexuality; but in the novels of this earlier period, in which he is reencountering his boyhood, sexuality leads to adulthood which leads to diminished psychological resources and death.

Coincidental with King's emphasis on the child and the boy is his emphasis on the family (often in a pathological phase). One of the earliest and most powerful of these novels is *The Shining*, which, long before systems theory, dramatized the point that the pathological individual is a symptom of the pathological family and that both must undergo treatment. Jack Torrance's obsessions and his wife's posture as victim are inheritances from their parents which bind them together and threaten Danny. In *Christine*, Arnie's pathological family environment leads to his destruction and theirs, while Dennis's family supports and creates him in its image. *It* provides the reader with a wide range of family dynamics, both successful and unsuccessful, and relates such to the girl and boys who are the protagonists. The most powerful of the numerous family novels is the tragic *Pet Sematary*, which develops for the reader a realistically ideal family which is demolished by its own estimable values when its child is senselessly killed. The question posed by the novel is whether the family can survive the death of a child. The answer is no. In this system, the death of a child kills the family.

THE WRITER AS HERO AND VILLAIN

A subject as close to King as the child and the family is that of the writer—a character who dominates as either protagonist or antagonist in a wide range of short stories, novellas, and novels (most significantly *'Salem's Lot*, *The Shining*, *It*, *Misery*, *The Tommyknockers*, and *The Dark Half*). The novelist-protagonist who dominates *'Salem's Lot* is more a product of King's youthful ideals than his experience. Like King, Ben Mears (a "mirror") undertakes a novel which will allow him to productively relive his childhood. But Ben's conflict with the vampire Barlow enlarges him to mythic proportions: as the personae about him converge and provide him understanding, faith, wisdom, and imagination, he develops a godlike perception and power. Metaphorically, when he encounters and conquers the vampire that is feeding on the town, he becomes the archetype of an elemental "good . . . whatever moved the greatest wheels of the universe." The following novel, *The Shining*, establishes balance by becoming an exact opposite to its predecessor: the alcoholic Torrance (a playwright this time) is the monster. King sees this particular writer as a failure because he stops writing—Torrance's writing block leads to psychosis. Among the complex communities of *The Stand*, a similar opposition is in the contrast between Larry (the successful musician) with

Harold (the unsuccessful writer): although his success nearly destroys him, Larry literally enacts a second crucifixion that saves the world; abnegating art for dark vision, Harold still manages some dignity before succumbing to demonic forces. Both figures physically resemble King: Larry has King's height and current physique and Harold has the height and King's adolescent physique. Although the hero is blond and the villain dark-haired, both have hair the quality of King's. In *It*, where the child's imagination is the only weapon of the adult against the death and meaninglessness of the eponymous evil, the novelist Bill Denbrough (who this time resembles Peter Straub) regains this state most easily and thus is a vital element of the protagonistic band.

Balancing again, King writes two novels—*Misery* and *The Tommyknockers*—which countervail such optimistic authorial characterizations. In *Misery* the primary subject is the negative relationship of the reader and the writer: the reader is the writer's enemy. Readers regularly read the genre writer rather than the literary artist—in *Misery*, this is the Gothic novelist. Since the readers' choice enforces conventions and confines the writer's creative talent, in a sense the audience "writes" the genre novel. Apparently tiring of these limitations, King personifies his tyrannical audience in the archetypal figure of Annie, who literally limits the aspiring literary artist, Paul Sheldon, to genre fiction by drugs, bondage, and torture. Despite such a negative response to whether readers are the motivation for writing, King gives the issue a serious and detailed treatment: his writing of a Gothic romance novel within a realistic novel and his exploration of the psychological processes of writers and their relationship with those of readers is a fascinating and original effort. And, again, he negates his own negation by undercutting Paul's distaste for genre fiction by his admiration for this bloodily extracted romance, even though its creation mutilated him.

While *Misery* suggests that the literary artist's social influence is more negligible than that of a genre novelist by creating a character with a conflicting literary agenda, *The Tom-myknockers* approaches the same issue by creating two authors: (1) the genre novelist, Bobbi Anderson, whose dark vision unleashes an alien presence which enslaves her community; and (2) the literary artist, poet Jim Gardener, whose self-sacrifice saves that community. Both are competent and dedicated writers who hold one another's work in esteem. But both are fatally flawed. Bobbi's kind of writing leaves her psychologically open to outside control (from audience and alien): she becomes the conduit which unearths and directs a cosmic darkness to the human community. Jim is armed against such possession, but isolated from the community by an art aspiring to the ideal. He has the vision to see through the darkness—he can and does die for the community, but it will never buy his books. As in *Misery*, King's final position on the writer's value is extremely pessimistic.

MASCULINITY, FEMININITY, AND MIDLIFE CRISIS

After writing *Misery* and *The Tommyknockers*, King entered a hiatus. For him, writing had become an existential act. He had the money but he felt controlled and depleted by the audience that he did have and despaired of the existence of any other kind of audience. Why continue to write? Developmental theory, such as Gail Sheehy's *Passages*, suggests that other processes were affecting King. He was passing through a chronological period from the age of 38 to 42 in which a man or woman working in the public area generally experiences extreme conflict as life takes a new direction: he or she reaches the end of a horizontal direction in which new territory and material are claimed through a process of conflict (a masculine direction), and a vertical direction where depth rather than width is sought through the development of nurturance and personal relationships (a feminine direction).

King emerged from his hiatus with an ambitious contract for four books—he wrote five (the last two of which were novels solely about women). But before he undertook this feminine direction, he closed the canon to children, Castle Rock, and writers. Children had by this time become lesser characters. The people of Castle Rock, given a slight nudge by a minor demon, destroyed themselves in the apocalyptic cataclysm ending *Needful Things*. The resolution of the issue of the writer in *The Dark Half* was more complex. The opposition of popular writer and artist in *Misery* and *The Tommyknockers* is here internalized in *The Dark Half*: warring for the soul of a writer are his personae as literary artist (Thad Beaumont) and as genre novelist (George Stark). The artist wins, but the victory is pyrrhic. Closer examination reveals that Beaumont's friends, wife, and children are psychologically akin to his nemesis. We find out in the sequel, *Needful Things*, that not only has the artist lost friends and family, but also the will to write. He is an alcoholic and the circle is closed. King leaves the issue behind him unresolved: it is what it is.

In *Gerald's Game* and *Dolores Claiborne*, King picks up a gauntlet. Long criticized for unidimensional female characters in such articles as Mary Pharr's "Partners in the *Danse*: Women in Stephen King's Fiction," he apparently decided that a new direction for growth both as human and as artist would be appropriate in accepting the challenge to create convincing women. Written simultaneously, the novels are most productively regarded as two poles in a meta-narrative process. At the one pole is the heroine of *Gerald*, Jessie Burlingame—economically and socially privileged, childless, and in her own eyes significant only as her husband's sexual object. At the other pole is Dolores, a figure apparently based on King's mother (to whom he dedicates the novel)—economically and socially underprivileged, a mother, and in her own eyes significant in herself. Through their telepathic awareness of one another and through their experience of the same eclipse as a central incident in their lives, King establishes the commonality of these two very different women: it lies in the fact that they are whole only in those years before and after men entered their lives—the period of the eclipse.

In *Gerald*, King dramatizes the entry of Jessie into an eclipse through the seduction and domination by her father; she exits the eclipse by killing her dominating husband, Gerald. The subsequent fragmenting of her victim persona into a community of sustaining female personae provides her with the resources to free herself from a literal bondage. In *Dolores*, the titular figure is a mother and wife who exits the eclipse by murdering a husband who also seeks to sexually exploit his daughter. In either case, the women experience one horror in common: the entry of men and sexuality into their lives. By erecting such contrasting poles as Jessie and Dolores, and yet maintaining both as sympathetic characters with a shared dilemma, King writes paired novels sympathetic to a wide spectrum of women and evades an easy condemnation of his women characters as unidimensional.

A Quest for Understanding

Overall, King's canon is a quest. But his battle cry is not "excelsior!" The direction is downwards and the path is a spiral. Many of King's characters experience life as a quest: Ben Mears of *'Salem's Lot* questing for self and conquering the vampire; *The Tommyknockers'* Gardener questing for death and finding self; the comrades of *The Stand* marching against the Dark One and founding the New Jerusalem; the boys of *It* killing fear; and the boys of *The Talisman* killing death. The gunslinger of *The Dark Tower* series is, however, probably most typical of King: he seeks to understand what the quest itself is. His enemies become his friends, his guides his traitors, his victims those he has saved, and his now a then. Paradox; transformation; balancing the dualities, an emergent, tenuous, ever-fading, and ever-appearing balance—these are the duplicitous landmarks in the terrain of King's work and his life. Both are open enough and fluent enough to mirror us and ours as we seek to make our own accommodations with modern monsters, personal meaninglessness, social chaos, physical decay, and death.

Stephen King's Gothic Melodrama

James Egan

In the nineteenth century, the novel, still a relatively modern literary form, established its respectability with the rise of realism. Practitioners of realism—who included Gustave Flaubert and Emile Zola in France, George Eliot and Thomas Hardy in England, Leo Tolstoy and Ivan Turgenev (and to a lesser degree, Fyodor Dostoyevsky) in Russia, and Herman Melville and Sarah Orne Jewett in the United States—eschewed sensationalism, supernaturalism, and sentimentality to create fictive worlds whose nuance, detail, and even monotony strove to mirror reality as faithfully as did that burgeoning art, photography. Novels that failed to meet the criteria of realism were relegated to vulgar, marginal status and considered more cheap entertainment than art. Gothic novels featured brooding landscapes and supernatural plots, while melodrama, a term derived from popular theater, denoted sensationalistic stories and one-dimensional characters. Both styles were held in the lowest literary repute, where they remained through much of the following century until the advent of postmodernism, a movement that called on scholars to question the previously unassailable categories dividing "high" and "popular" art.

Thus, as James Egan demonstrates in the following selection, to examine the gothic and melodramatic elements at play in Stephen King's fiction is not to denigrate his work but, rather, to view it as part of a tradition that has existed, however often ignored, for more than two hundred years. Egan points out elements of King's plots and characterizations—his exploration of the irrational and unknow-

James Egan, "A Single Powerful Spectacle: Stephen King's Gothic Melodrama," *Extrapolation*, vol. 27, Spring 1986, pp. 62–75. Copyright © 1986 by Kent State University Press. Reproduced by permission.

able, his use of violence and the grotesque—that derive from established gothic and melodramatic conventions. Just as important, Egan claims, are King's innovations, especially through his allusions to late-twentieth-century pop culture and his incorporation of aspects of the political novel. These particular stylistic traits, so characteristic of King, distinguish him not only from his nineteenth-century gothic and melodramatic predecessors but also from his contemporaries in the horror genre.

James Egan is a professor of English at the University of Akron. He is a widely published specialist in seventeenth-century literature as well as in the gothic, science fiction, and fantasy genres.

The Gothic tradition which has survived into the twentieth century, after passing through the hands of the Gothic dramatists, Mary Shelley, Bram Stoker, Henry James, and Shirley Jackson, has evolved into a complex mixture of the sensational, the sentimental, the melodramatic, and the formulaic. True, a Gothic work such as Jackson's *The Haunting of Hill House* (1959) occasionally achieves belletristic status, but most examples of the genre can be appropriately categorized as "popular" fiction. Stephen King's numerous references and allusions make plain his familiarity with the Gothic tradition, particularly that part which begins with the publication of *Frankenstein.* One finds in King many Gothic conventions of setting, plot, characterization, and theme, along with an assortment of melodramatic techniques which accentuate his Gothic motifs and help to shape the world view which permeates his fiction. It must be emphasized, however, that the Gothic and the melodramatic in King are virtually inseparable, just as they are in the Gothic tradition itself. Equally important, one must recognize that King employs the Gothic and the melodramatic in accordance with the demands of popular formula literature, for he intends to offer his readers a combination of stock thrills and intriguing innovations, the security of the familiar and the unsettling delights of the unknown.

VICE, VIOLENCE, AND DERANGEMENT

As Elizabeth MacAndrew has argued, Gothic literature highlights vice. King treats vice consistently, luridly, graphically. One of the main plots of *The Dead Zone* (1979) details the exploits of Frank Dodd, a rapist-murderer who stalks a succession of young women and ends his spree with the killing of a nine-year-old. Dodd's behavior follows the strangely consistent pattern of the deranged mind, a pattern which King describes in detail. After slapping a victim around and then raping her, Dodd savors the joy of murder: "He began to throttle [Alma Frechette], yanking her head up from the bandstand's board flooring and then slamming it back down. Her eyes bulged. Her face went pink, then red, then congested purple. Her struggles began to weaken." Eventually, the novel's psychic detective, John Smith, identifies Dodd; but Dodd declines to surrender quietly. Instead, he cuts his throat with a razor blade, spraying a bathroom with blood, and hangs around his neck "a sign crayoned in lipstick. It read: I CONFESS." Several humans confront a huge, rabid St. Bernard in *Cujo* (1981). Cujo mauls Joe Camber and his friend, Gary Pervier, and traps Donna Trenton and her son, Tad, in Donna's car. King devotes a substantial section of the novel to the brutal, life-or-death struggle between Donna and Cujo. The dog bites her, and she in turn slams the car door repeatedly on the dog's head. For melodramatic effect, this war of attrition goes on in nearly unbearable heat and humidity, conditions which cause Tad to go into convulsions and finally contribute to his death. More than a rabid animal, Cujo is evil, a demonic reincarnation of Dodd returned to prey on the innocent once again. Sex competes with violence in *Cujo* as Steve Kemp, Donna's rejected lover, vandalizes her home while she battles the dog. Kemp's orgiastic violence does additional duty as a symbolic rape: sexually aroused, he nearly demolishes the Trenton home and then masturbates on Donna's bed.

Sex and violence also combine sensationally in *Firestarter* (1980). John Rainbird, a bizarre, deformed hit-man for The Shop, a shadowy government espionage agency, strangles his victims slowly, hoping to witness death as they draw their last breaths. After learning of Charlie McGee, the adolescent girl with pyrokinetic abilities, he becomes fascinated with the child's power and personality. Rainbird wants to become "intimate" with Charlie—he seems to have fallen in love with her. His grotesque appearance and peculiar intentions evoke the stereotype of the child molester. Gruesome destruction is panoramic in *Carrie* (1974). Following repeated harassment by her mother and her peers, Carrie White turns her telekinetic powers on the town of Chamberlain: water mains explode, gasoline stations erupt into flames, and the population stumbles about in a state of chaos—all of this because Carrie has become a vindictive, seemingly demonic character who seeks revenge on each and every one of her tormentors and even upon those who did not harm her. Once a victim, Carrie evolves into a methodical executioner whose vendetta takes up the final third of the novel. Doubt and guilt do not impede Carrie, who simply kills whomever she chooses. The novel shifts, with melodramatic rapidity, from Carrie the victim to Carrie the avenger.

INNOCENCE AND EVIL

King's emphasis on blood and gore does not always depend upon vice, however. *The Breathing Method*, one of four novellas included in *Different Seasons* (1982), qualifies as a "tale of the uncanny" told at a mysterious gentlemen's club in New York. Miss Standfield, an unwed pregnant woman who has diligently practiced controlled breathing in order to make delivery easier, is beheaded in a traffic accident while on the way to the hospital to give birth. Her body, though, remains alive, and the narrator, Dr. McCarron, helps the "corpse" deliver its child. But McCarron's excursion into the supernatural has not yet ended, for as he prepares to leave. Miss Standfield's head "mouthed four words: *Thank you, Dr. McCarron.*" McCarron informs the head that Miss Standfield has delivered a boy, and the head obligingly dies. The determined innocent-in-distress, Miss Standfield, has heroically, melodramatically, cheated fate and triumphed against all odds. Though diversified, the incidents cited above all emphasize "violence, physical disaster, and emotional agony" which is both Gothic and melodramatic. King starkly polarizes and exaggerates innocence and malignancy for intensified emotional effect.

King's drastic, violent subject matter fits in with his essentially Gothic themes. He stresses the primordial power and pervasiveness of the unknown, the irrationality and unpredictability of the human psyche, and the moral reality of good and evil. King's metaphysics of the Dark Fantastic provides a contemporary rendering of concepts that have permeated Gothicism for more than two centuries. King treats the Dark Fantastic as an environment where the primitive, superstition, and rudimentary incarnations of good and evil hold sway. In such an environment, those who refuse to take the fantastic seriously or who continue to explain it in terms of the realistic are usually its victims. How valid, King asks, are the empirical and psychological paradigms upon which contemporary society relies to explain reality? And what of the nature of reality itself? Should one conclude that reality is chaotic and menacing? Can subjective phenomena such as the Dark Fantastic be understood objectively? King makes, moreover, a highly plausible assertion about the relationship of the known to the unknown: the territory of the unknown is immense and probably expanding, not diminishing, despite the increasing sophistication of modern investigative methods. Since King deals with the volatile, explosive behavioral eruptions are to be expected. The plot, characterization, rhetoric, and world view of his fiction support these thematic premises and may be viewed, in melodramatic terms, as vehement arguments for them.

KING'S USES OF MELODRAMA

Critical consensus holds that melodrama stresses plot over character, plot which relies considerably upon coincidence and accident. Melodramatic plots feature rapid movements from one crisis to another and frequently terminate in death crises, or they accentuate "crucial times in life that seem to determine one's fate once and for all." King's characteristically fast-moving and episodic plots often depend upon coincidence to link together a series of crises which hinge on or end in death. He builds *The Stand* (1978) around several subplots which trace the lives of half a dozen people who try to survive a plague that destroys virtually the entire population of the earth. In order to survive, the main characters must surmount disaster after disaster. Above all, they must avoid the Dark Man, Randall Flagg, and finally confront him—in each case they are at risk. Everyone encounters hazards in the form of emotional agony, encounters with death or near misses, and the need to kill. Nick Andros loses his lover, Rita, to a drug overdose, Mother Abagail must stare down Flagg's menacing animal familiars on a lonely Nebraska road, and Harold Lauder must deal with maddening jealousy after the woman he loves rejects him for another. *The Stand* ends in a holocaust when an atomic bomb destroys Flagg's assembled forces. *The Dead Zone* opens with the protagonist's dangerous fall while ice skating as a youth, proceeds to an auto accident which leaves him in a coma for five years, and then traces his encounters with a rapist-murderer. Before the novel closes, he tries to assassinate a diabolical politician, only to be shot in the attempt. One seldom finds a dull—or normal—moment. Clearly, much of what happens to Smith seems accidental or coincidental, particularly his astounding awakening and apparently full recovery from a lengthy coma.

King uses a variety of specific plot devices, moreover, to keep the level of suspense high in his crisis fiction. Short, fast-paced, rapidly changing scenes are commonplace, notably in *'Salem's Lot* (1975), *The Stand*, and *The Shining* (1977). Though his novels tend to be long, he breaks narrative detail down into many miniature, self-contained episodes, a favorite tactic of melodramatists. Multiple narrative viewpoints are another suspense tactic. In *The Stand* and *'Salem's Lot* he tells the story from the vantage points of many characters, often switching points of view as he changes chapters. The effect is both panoramic and provocative because important details are provided in small increments.

King likewise creates suspense with the thriller tactic of ending chapters on a climactic high note which whets the reader's curiosity, or by providing clues and hints which create a state of nervous anticipation. As it draws to a close, *The Shining* evolves into a continuous chase scene, a suspense device in itself. Danny Torrance has, in fact, been the object of a chase since the novel opened. An early chapter ends with Danny being stung by wasps while he sleeps, another when the ghost of Room 217 tries to strangle him, and a third when the hedge animals pursue him through the snow to the front porch of the Overlook Hotel. The suspense generated at the end of each chapter holds the reader's attention: one grows more curious about who or what will be Danny's final pursuer. King fancies murder-mystery plots and effectively utilizes the suspense inherent in such plots. In *Cujo*, Donna Trenton and her son turn up missing and the planting of clues begins. The police discover Donna's car has vanished, Vic Trenton tells them about the taunting note he received from Donna's ex-lover, Steve Kemp, and the police soon apprehend Kemp. Once the clues rest in the hands of the authorities, the reader waits eagerly for them to deduce that Donna took the car to Joe Camber's garage for repairs and wonders how long it will take for her to be rescued from Cujo.

GOTHIC THRILLS AND NEUROSES

An equally important way of creating thrills is intrinsic to the Gothic genre itself. The deliberate, necessary blurring of appearance and reality in most of King's fiction keeps the reader uncertain and therefore attentive to plot developments. In *The Mist* (1980) a group of people huddles inside a supermarket while an impenetrable, acrid mist blankets the world outside and carnivorous creatures prowl around. What the creatures may be, where they came from, how they might behave, and the extent to which insanity has infected those inside the market are all uncertain matters. The ambiguity of the situation makes distinctions between truth and falsehood problematical at best. A similar motif appears in *'Salem's Lot*—the Lot has been invaded by a vampire and his familiar. Is an "invasion" by a vampire possible, or no more than a mass hallucination? If vampires are real, might they be killed by the methods folklore prescribes? Who faces the greatest danger from the undead? Few of these questions allow for definite answers and suspense grows out of the uncertainty.

A final suspense gambit, clearly a stock melodramatic one, consists of delaying the "inevitable and wholly foreseen" denouement Perhaps King's clearest and most emphatic use of this tactic occurs in *Christine* (1982), the story of a 1958 Plymouth inhabited by the demonic spirit of its former owner, Roland LeBay. Arnie Cunningham, a lonely, socially isolated teenager, becomes frenzied as soon as he passes LeBay's house and notices the car for sale. It becomes apparent from the outset that Christine has a relentless supernatural grip on Arnie and that he will readily do her bidding. The plot makes it equally clear that Arnie's closest friend, Dennis Guilder, suspects and fears Christine's malign influence. A romantic and a revenge plot intervene, but the denouement methodically arrives: Christine turns Arnie into it human lackey and Dennis finally succeeds in destroying the evil machine.

King's emphasis on fast-moving, thrilling plots moves his work in the direction of another melodramatic convention, allegorically simple good and evil characters whose appearances correspond with their inner natures. He typically delineates such characters, moreover, as extremes of vice or virtue, freely adopting the Gothic convention that neurotic and obsessional emotional dynamics are the aspects of a character's psyche to be stressed, in addition to the Gothic preoccupation with guilt, fear, and madness. His characters act more out of compulsion than out of free choice. Like many other melodramatists, King plays up the consistent dual result of compulsion: victimization by a variety of aggressors, including nature, society and evil individuals, and subsequent aggression. Finally, characterization in King fits in with the traditional melodramatic striving after pathetic effects. Jack Torrance, protagonist-turned-antagonist of *The Shining*, suffers from a variety of unresolved psychological problems, including memories of a family-abusing father; alcoholism, and an explosive temper. When he arrives at the Overlook, Jack is driven to discover its dark secrets by his inner demons of guilt, paranoia, and self-destructiveness. These inner demons join forces with the demons who inhabit the Overlook to transform Jack into a victim and then into an aggressor. The amount of free will he possesses remains open to serious question from the story's outset.

VICTIMS AND VILLAINS

King portrays Carrie White as a victim from early childhood until death. Denied a normal maturation and social life by her mother's religious fanaticism, she becomes the perpetual butt of jokes and harbors fantasies of vengeance against her many tormentors. After Carrie's humiliation at the prom, fantasies evolve into aggressive obsessions, and then into overt madness during her telekinetic vendetta against Chamberlain. Surely madness compromises the matter of free will, yet Carrie's dilemma loses none of its pathos. The reader can easily sympathize with her because of her frustrated, empty life and because she possesses powers which mystify and perhaps control her. Carrie's vendetta, of course, also creates sympathy for the innocent victims who must pay for her lifetime of deprivation. Driven by a messianic desire to save civilization, John Smith in *The Dead Zone* has the ability to "see" the future. But his second sight reveals to him only the dark side of awareness—he can predict what will be, but can rarely convince others. A melodramatic simplicity stands out in Smith's character when King plays him off against his two primary antagonists, a rapist-murderer and a ruthless politician—obviously society can only profit from his exposure of these evildoers. Still, society refuses to listen, preferring to suspect Smith and his "gift." This pariah-like treatment intensifies Smith's obsession to carry out his quest, and pathos mixes with irony as he pushes onward to save his uncaring fellow man. Predictably, Smith dies as he lived, only vaguely aware of the mysterious forces which drive his personality. He does not pause for detailed reflection. He acts.

The single-natured yet relatively complex villain acts as the moving force in melodrama generally, and in Gothic melodrama demonic-seeming villains predominate. King's villains blend into the tradition of Gothic melodrama: monopathic, relentless, obsessed, they are his most fully realized and intriguing characters. Randall Flagg is literally a demon, a shape-shifter who can become a man, an animal, or a disembodied force. Evil displays itself in Flagg's very appearance, for those who dream of him see only a faceless man. Though Flagg may be surrounded by a supporting cast of criminals and semi-demons. he has no rival as *The Stand*'s most interesting villain. Harold Lauder and Nadine Cross rediscover a truism, that all who serve Flagg eventually become his pawns. The Dark Man's cruelty knows no limits: he crucifies his victims, turns them into slobbering imbeciles, or hurls them from the upper floors of buildings. He broods endlessly over his relentless ambition to destroy his enemies in Boulder, led by the saintly Mother Abagail, and works tirelessly to build an arsenal. Both demon and workaholic,

Flagg eventually falls victim to another melodramatic convention, namely that "Evil can only destroy itself, no matter how hard it tries." John Rainbird, the huge, grotesquely scarred Indian of *Firestarter*, looms as the most physically conspicuous Gothic villain in King's fiction. His sinister freakishness evokes pathos when he encounters Charlie McGee, the innocent adolescent heroine. Here, beyond doubt, appearances alone are reliable measures of good and evil. Rainbird lives for a single purpose, to kill, doing so with ingenuity and pleasure. A creature of almost pure malignancy, monopathic, devoid of qualities higher than a powerful survival instinct, Rainbird dominates the novel. Before Andy and Charlie McGee can escape from The Shop, they must confront him, must either destroy him or be destroyed.

WOMEN, CHILDREN, AND THE ELDERLY

In constant danger themselves, women in Gothic melodrama often become a source of danger to others as well. King follows this convention of characterization closely, establishing his female characters, for the most part, as vulnerable stereotypes in order to make the convention operate more effectively. Soon after the Torrance family's arrival at the Overlook. Wendy turns into a target of Jack's mania. In order to fight back, she jeopardizes Danny by using him as a psychological weapon or a bargaining chip. Susan Norton, a heroine-turned-predator in *'Salem's Lot*, is coveted by the vampire Barlow. Susan signals danger for the novel's two main protagonists, Ben and Mark, because of her close relationship with both before she became a vampire. Fran Goldsmith of *The Stand* suffers as the object of Harold Lauder's unrequited love. Even though she finds Lauder's diary and realizes that he plans revenge by killing Stu Redman, her new lover, she cannot determine where and when Lauder will strike, or whether he intends to kill her also. In the end, Fran becomes both victim and threat when Lauder decides to retaliate by detonating a hidden bomb at a meeting of the Boulder citizens' council where Stu will be present; not surprisingly, several innocent people perish. Women, then, generally serve as targets of villainy and objects of pathos so that King's male villains can remain the most powerful figures and the initiators of his fiction's primary action.

Small children and elderly people, Michael Booth argues, serve to "reinforce pathetic effects" in melodrama, and this is their primary purpose in King's fiction. The theme of virtue in distress, a convention of the sentimental novel, King applies primarily to children. Tad Trenton in *Cujo* surely merits pity because he is at the mercy of a panoply of forces he cannot understand: hunger, thirst, a distressed mother, a rabid dog, and supernatural powers. Billy Drayton's position in *The Mist* offers little improvement. The boy has lost his mother, gotten trapped in a crowd of increasingly demented strangers, and been singled out as a sacrificial offering to propitiate carnivorous beasts. Charlie McGee's dilemma may be the most pitiable of all, for she is "gifted" with pyrokinesis, a talent which causes her endless anxiety. If pyrokinesis itself were not problem enough, The Shop captures and uses her as a psychological guinea pig, John Rainbird lusts after her, and she must use her "gift" to kill nearly the entire staff at The Shop's compound. King's child characters are purposely one-dimensional, stereotypical innocents-in-distress whose misfortunes invariably invoke pity. He treats the elderly in similar fashion—for example, Jud Crandall in *Pet Sematary*, Matt Burke in *'Salem's Lot*, and Mother Abagail in *The Stand*, each of whom faces a hazardous situation, a superior human opponent, or the supernatural. Like the children, these three must cope with complex problems alone, and their physical infirmities parallel the physical immaturity of the children. Pathos arises from the reader's fear that the older people, despite their heroic efforts, cannot finally escape the status of dependents. When the elderly die at the villain's hands or in the battle against him, however, they at least assure themselves of the mildly heroic stature reserved for virtuous characters in the sentimental tradition.

RHETORICAL STYLE

King relies upon bombastic rhetoric, a fundamental part of Gothic melodrama, to underscore the effects of his plotting and characterization. In the following passage from *'Salem's Lot*, Straker, the human familiar of the vampire Barlow, has just strung young Mark Petrie from a ceiling beam to wait for Barlow's return. Straker cannot resist teasing his victim: "You're trembling, young master . . . your flesh is white—but it will be whiter! Yet you need not be so afraid. My Master has the capacity for kindness. . . . There is only a little sting, like the doctor's needle, and then sweetness. . . . You will go see your father and mother, yes? You will see them after they sleep." This sarcastic gloating naturally encourages the reader's sympathy for the helpless boy, and emotions polarize, the normal effect of bombast. Straker's bombast echoes the good-evil dichotomies found elsewhere in the novel, the juxtaposition of totally negative and purely positive. Carrie White's mother indulges in an equally blatant outburst when she tries to discourage Carrie from making a dress for the prom: "'Take it off, Carrie. We'll go down and burn it in the incinerator together, and then pray for forgiveness. We'll do penance.' Her eyes began to sparkle with the strange, disconnected zeal that came over her at events which she considered to be tests of faith. 'I'll stay home from work and you'll stay home from school. We'll pray. We'll ask for a Sign. We'll get us down on our knees and ask for the Pentecostal fire.'" Anything but subtle, Mrs. White's diatribe provokes confrontation, as melodramatic bombast usually does. Rhetoric magnifies the emotional conflicts that divide Carrie and her mother, branding Mrs. White as the aggressor and Carrie as the victim. Predictably, her mother's bluntly emotional appeal prompts Carrie to make an emphatically emotional response—a direct, uncompromising denial.

King's handling of subject matter, plot, characterization, and rhetoric implies a world view consistent with the world view of melodrama. Melodrama emphasizes the equitable rewarding of virtue and punishment of vice, and perpetuates the "fantasy of a world that operates according to our heart's desires." Since melodrama sets before us a world of clarity, simplicity, either-or dichotomies, and absolutes, appearance and reality conveniently correspond. Melodrama stresses as well fate and fate's victims. Whether or not fate figures as a cosmic culprit, melodrama encourages pity for victims and outrage at evildoers. Several of King's theories about horror fiction align themselves with the melodramatic world view. A major purpose of such fiction, he asserts, is to "confirm our own good feelings about the status quo by showing us extravagant visions of what the alternative might be." The writer of horror fiction functions, therefore, as "an agent of the status quo," the norm operating according to what could be construed as a fantasy of a universe governed according to certain fixed principles. Horror stories, he argues, are "conservative," essentially the same as the morality plays of earlier centuries. In effect, horror stories, like other species of melodrama, support a conventional morality. The horror story's "strict moralities," in fact, make it a "reaffirmation of life and good will and simple imagination." King defines the horror story, finally, as an "invitation to lapse into simplicity," a definition which supports the melodramatic preoccupation with absolutes, extremes, dichotomies.

King's fictive practices confirm his belief in the world view of melodrama. Sensationalistic vice tends to be punished grimly: John Rainbird is incinerated, Randall Flagg flees to the nether world, and Jack Torrance forfeits his soul to the transcendent evil of the Overlook. Although not all of King's villains are punished so drastically, their ends are invariably frustrated. As demonstrated earlier, the innocent suffer abundantly, but suffering frequently vindicates their purity or rightness. This premise seems particularly true of child characters. Mark Petrie of *'Salem's Lot* believes in the supernatural and in vampire lore, a belief shared by few of the adults he deals with. Mark loses his parents, his friends and nearly his life; however, his suspicions finally prove correct. John Smith of *The Dead Zone*, a childlike adult, undergoes a similar experience: the well-meaning Smith meets with recurring skepticism and frustration. Yet, in the book's climactic confrontation scene his suspicions about Gregg Stillson are justified—Stillson reveals his villainy when he holds a child in front of him to ward off Smith's bullets. King's dependence upon stereotypical figures, moreover, reinforces a world view that accentuates absolutes, clarity, and simplicity. Since characters are usually delineated as extremes of good or bad, reader recognition of a particular character's nature, motivations, and values rarely proves difficult. Again, in view of the one-dimensional nature of characters, the changes they undergo are easily anticipated and not unduly complex. Nothing will cause a Stillson or a Barlow, for example, to relent in his pursuit of a singular, clearly announced goal. King also provides clarity by means of his characters' preferences for immediate, direct action over lengthy, involved introspection. The major decisions they make often take on an either-or simplicity. All characters in *The Stand*, major or minor, must choose between the goodness of Mother Abagail and the evil of the Dark Man—the moral middle ground quickly vanishes for both character and reader. The bombastic rhetoric to which King's villains, particularly, seem addicted further illustrates the world of moral and psychological extremes in which they function. Bombast reduces potentially complex issues to simple, emotionally charged ones, establishing morally convenient polarizations. Plot, finally, moves so rapidly from crisis to crisis that it traps characters in the identities they assume early in a story. This crisis plotting necessitates limited, often fated characters who change little, irrespective of the dilemmas that assail them. Though it often appears to generate ambiguity, plotting probably resolves at least as much ambiguity as it creates.

An accomplished melodramatic strategist, King understands horror fiction's formulaic nature and that a formula writer must blend conventions with inventions. His Gothic melodrama provides the "emotional security" inherent in anticipated, standardized subject matter, settings, character and plot types, and themes, while the exciting effects he seeks often derive from his innovative experiments with the familiar. As suggested earlier, King evokes horror and fear by treating a variety of sensational subject matter: gruesome deaths, torture, sexual aberrations, grave-robbing, a worldwide plague, and the like. He offers a haunted house in *'Salem's Lot*, a haunted hotel in *The Shining*, and a wide range of demons, vampires, monstrous, quasi-human villains, and occult powers. Ventures into the unknown, his plots dramatize confrontations with immanent evil, the dark side of the human psyche, and with transcendent evil, the unfathomable mysterium.

CHAPTER 3

Reading the Books

The Stand's All-American Apocalypse

Joseph Reino

The Stand, first published in 1978 and reissued in unexpurgated form in 1990, is King's longest novel. The original version was more than eight hundred pages, the reissue more than eleven hundred pages. As critic Joseph Reino points out in the following selection, *The Stand* is also among King's most ambitious books in terms of thematic and philosophical scope. It describes an epic battle of good versus evil set in a postapocalyptic world. The vast majority of the world's population has died from a "superflu" accidentally released from a U.S. government bio-weapons lab, and the survivors divide into camps of good (headed by saintly Mother Abagail) and evil (led by diabolical Randall Flagg).

Reino explores the Judeo-Christian mythical themes that are interwoven in the novel. Biblical evocations of the end of the world coexist in *The Stand* with themes and attitudes that derive from the 1960s counterculture and Vietnam-era conflict. *The Stand* envisions a future in which the fruits of progress are desolation and tyranny. Even though Reino appreciates the complexity of King's epic mythology and range of reference, he finds the novel's parts generally superior to its whole, deeming the novel too long even in its original 1978 form. Nonetheless, *The Stand* remains a favorite among King's many fans.

Joseph Reino has published widely on Stephen King. He has also published scholarship on Saint Augustine.

The main character in *The Stand* is not human, but rather a highly contagious flulike disease, nicknamed "Captain Trips"—

Joseph Reino, *Stephen King: The First Decade,* Carrie *to* Pet Sematary. Boston: Twayne Publishers, 1988. Copyright © 1988 by G.K. Hall & Co. Reproduced by permission.

a superflu that almost totally wipes out the population of the United States in the year 1985, seven years after the publication of the novel. The deadly epidemic results from a scientific experiment in which lethal viruses are accidentally released into the atmosphere. One of the characters describes it this way: "Your somebody in authority got a bunch of bacteriologists, virologists, and epidemiologists together in some government installation to see how many funny bugs they could dream up. And they dreamed up a dilly." Book 1 of this tripartite, quasi-epic narrative—epic in its eight-hundred-page length, if in nothing else—deals with the consequences of this scientific disaster, and is dated 16 June–4 July 1985. The 1985 date follows chronologically that of George Orwell's *1984* (1948), when the earth is in the total control of Big Brother and freedom of thought and action, once inspired by the Declaration of Independence and the American Constitution, are completely annihilated. While the Orwell novel plays no role in *The Stand*, King actually extends the devastation from the cruel 1984 politics of Orwell's novel to the crassly mismanaged 1985 biology of his own. Yet the elaborate attempt to restore American democracy in the face of universal death and devastation can be considered a response to Orwell, expressing an unusual note of confidence in the lasting values of the American political system.

STAR-SPANGLED SYMBOLISM

The 4 July 1985 date that concludes book 1 is not without ironic significance nor lacking grotesquely comical aspects when one of the characters (sex-loose rock-star Larry Underwood) greets the morning of a 1985 Independence Day with a buck-naked, "bump-and-grind" burlesque-rendition of "The Star-Spangled Banner." What had been "proudly hailed" at the "twilight's last gleaming" by the woman with whom he was sharing a tight sleeping bag (Rita Blakemoor) was not the red-white-and-blue banner of the United States, but Underwood's "genital flag"—a piece of patriotic anatomy, though here flaunted and flagged about in an obviously undignified fashion that is not without importance to the flag symbolism (cf. the surname Flagg) of the novel. Interestingly, Karl Shapiro, in his novel *Edsel* (1971), also uses the flag and Independence Day symbolism in a sexual sense, when the quasi-impotent protagonist (college professor Edsel himself) finally achieves a successful orgasm to the tune of a star-spangled red, white and blue. In *The Stand*, however, the Fourth of July is also the day on which Larry Underwood, having slept with Rita Blakemoor, discovered she had overdosed and died in her sleep. In a sense, he has slept with a corpse.

THE SIGNIFICANCE OF NAMES

The highly contagious flu of *The Stand*, with a 99.4 percent communicability, was nick-named "Captain Trips" when it reached California—a name deriving from rock star Jerry Garcia of the "Grateful Dead," one of the leaders of the drug cult in the sixties—a nickname that appears glancingly in [King's] "Night Surf," where a similar devastating flu attack occurs. "Captain Trips" gives the novel, as well as the short story, important allegorical dimensions. For as drug trips go "tripping" across the United States (hypodermically from youth to youth), so the fatal disease goes "tripping" from person to person, both in novel and short story, with a death speed that turns out to be medically incredible. The devastating disease seems to express itself—sometimes actually personify itself—in the ominous figure of Randall Flagg, King's version of a pestilential Big Brother who is made to resemble both the superflu with its 99.4 percent communicability and the annihilating Antichrist of a two-thousand-year Christian tradition. Both Flagg and the imperious flu—to use the language of folklorists—were "shape-shifters." Usually on an *R-F* pattern, Randall Flagg randomly changed his name to Richard Fry, Robert Franq, Ramsey Forrest—though more often than not he is identified throughout *The Stand* as simply the "Walkin Dude." But even this *R-F* pattern is too localized and confining for the ubiquitous Flagg, and therefore the following more expansive suggestion is made: "Call him Beelzebub . . . Nyarlahotep, and Ahaz and Astaroth . . . R'yelah and Seti and Anubis." The unusual disease itself is described by one of the characters (George Richardson) in language that parodies his shape- and name-shifting behavior: "With Captain Trips, the flu *itself* changed every time your body came to a defense posture. And it just went on shifting from form to form until the body was worn out. The result, inevitably, was death." *The Stand* makes clear that there were those who believed that Randall Flagg, the "shape-changer" like A6, had "started the plague himself, that he was the Antichrist whose coming was foretold in Revelation." In fact, the "dark man is as real as the superflu itself, as real as the atomic bombs that still sit somewhere in their leadlined closets."

The deliberate interplay of the names "Trips" and "Walkin" (and later on "Trotts," as in Abigail Trotts) ought to be obvious enough, and the Dude's cross-country movements are emphasized, significantly, at opportune moments. The Dude's inexplicable peripatetics are first detailed in chapter 17 in rock song, refrainlike fashion: "the dark man strode south," "he walked rapidly," "he moved along, not pausing," "he strode on a steady, ground-eating pace." These rapid-walking movements are underscored with effectively used clocking and knocking images, monotonously and metronomically keeping time (whenever the Dude comes hurrying along), like an ominous bass rhythm to an evil melodic line. Thus, "he hammered along," "he rocked along, his feet easy in the boots which were comfortably sprung in all the right places," and "his . . . dusty boots clocking on the pavement." When he determines the destruction of one of his agents (Bobby Terry, for example), strange clock-rhythmic sounds are heard, "like rundown bootheels hammering swiftly along the secondary road macadams." When he appears to Judge Ferris as a crow—a creature he not only commands (like wolves) but also transforms himself into—he makes weird tap-tap-tap sounds upon the windowpane in the manner of Edgar Allan Poe's nevermore raven: "this *was* the dark man, his soul, his *ka* somehow projected into this raindrenched, grinning crow that was looking in at him, checking up on him," and the "crow leaned forward and, very deliberately, tapped on the glass." Clock images climax when one of the Dude's stooges finds "over a dozen five-and-dime plastic timers" to attach to his copper ignition system for the purpose of blowing up the enemies of Randall Flagg: "You set them for fifteen minutes or a half hour and when they got back to zero they went *ding* and you knew it was time to take your pie out of the oven. Only instead of going *ding* this time . . . they are going to go *bang*." All the numerous foot-clicking images appear to be setting up Randall Flagg as a doomsday clock for a world whose final hour is about to strike.

FLAGG AS HUMAN ANTICHRIST

Of the various traditional characteristics of the Antichrist (that he would be born in Bethlehem, reign from Jerusalem for three and a half years, rebuild the Temple of Solomon, and be received worldwide as the messiah), three interesting ones are emphasized in *The Stand*: the supernatural powers, the ability to levitate, and the divine pretensions. All are explored in unusual imaginative detail. Flagg is presented, for example, with the ability to "suddenly appear in a small, out-of-the-way burg" and "materialize like a ghost." When this ability to appear and disappear is combined with the ability to levitate, Randall Flagg then seems to blend into himself aspects of both human time and divine eternity.

With his ever-present sense of irony, however, King arranges an act of private levitation at a moment when the otherwise-perceptive Flagg suspects that he might have been making "stupid decisions" all along and thus abruptly "decided to push it all aside and levitate." This pseudodivine power always made him feel better: "looking out at the desert sky, he proclaims himself God by insistently repeating, *"I am, I am, I am, I AM."* But Flagg is immediately confronted with a succession of defeats, as when in an attempt to levitate, "it was a long, long time before his bootheels would leave the sundeck, and when they did they would only hover a quarter of an inch above the concrete."

Most unusual among the divine pretensions is Flagg's ability to send forth his "eye." According to the cosmology of Heliopolis in ancient Egypt (ca. 2780 B.C.), the primeval Atum, the single-armed deity who had self-generated out of a primeval mound, had the ability to send forth anywhere on the earth his single eye, known as the "Wedjet"—representing the Egyptian Mother Goddess in her destructive aspect. The technical, mythological name for the Egyptian eye, Wedjet, is never used in *The Stand*, but its search-and-seizure behavior ought to be clear enough to anyone familiar with that five-thousand-year-old mythology. Ancient Egyptian texts associate this primeval eye with terror, fright, slaughter, howling, and cringing, as in the spell that is #316 of the Egyptian Coffin texts.

With such gothic attributes, the ominous Wedjet is a perfect companion for the pseudodivine Flagg, who (probably like the reader) fails to understand the phenomenon: how, for example, he could have obtained such a detachable eye, or why he can use it. Its power is such that Flagg can throw a "sudden furious stare" at some wolves, and nearly a half a dozen would fall to fighting, "their gutteral sounds like ripping cloth in the stillness." But the real purpose of this traveling eye (that sometimes falls "mysteriously blind") is to spy out potential dangers to Flagg and his associates. Most significant among its traveling extravaganzas are the ability to overcome an eagle, a traditional medieval symbol of apocalyptic triumph of Christ ("The eagle fell almost all the way to the ground, stunned, before recovering itself"), and its corresponding inability to overcome a dog, the traditional gothic symbol of opposition to vampires. Despite its awesome power, the Wedjet too, like Randall Flagg himself, sometimes "flags"—a pun on his name that King himself occasionally uses, but a brief dialogue between Tom Collins and Stu Redman, toward the end of *The Stand*, seems to imply that the Walkin Dude, despite "flaggings," may come back.

FLAGG'S PSYCHOPATHIC HENCHMEN

Both the psychopathic killer Lloyd Henreid and the pyromaniac Trashcan Man (whose real name is Donald Merwin Elbert) not only wander in the long-cast shadows of Randall Flagg, but are psychopathic embodiments of his Antichrist spirit. If any two characters should have been destined for flu destruction by Captain Trips, certainly Lloyd Henreid and Trashcan Man should have, but atomic detonation alone seems to have the power to clean up the earth by eliminating them. As moral cleansing agents, mere diseases are too weak.

Even though he is supposed to be the frightening "man with no face," Randall Flagg is a mere symbolic abstraction by contrast with the hideous specifics of Lloyd Henreid, a "pusbag" of criminality, a "scummy douchebag," who is unable to catch a cold, to say nothing of the superflu itself, even when someone sneezes into his face, "spraying him with thick spit." His behavior in jail when all the "screws" around him are dying of superflu—that is, eating a cockroach, gnawing on the tail of a rat, negotiating the stiff body of his dead cellmate for future food ("Nothing personal, I ain't going to eat you, old buddy; not unless I have to")—is so revolting as to be barely repeatable. Firebug Donald Merwin Elbert, known as the "Trashcan Man" (whose curious nickname echoes Lloyd's prison companion's, "Trask") is an "unknowing soul brother." Drawn in a dream by the hypnotic powers of Flagg, "Trash" drags himself through Colorado's famous Eisenhower Tunnel, crying out repeatedly, "My life for you, my life for you."

Trash is offering his life to the "light" at the end of the tunnel of death, the "light" being both Flagg himself and Flagg's imaginary capital, the seven-in-one city of the promised, the fabled Cibola of Hispanic and Indian folklore. The legendary "Cibola" functions in Trash's imagination as a kind of infernal Jerusalem, a counterpart of the heavenly Jerusalem of Revelation 21:10–27, as Dante's infernal city of Dis is a counterpart of the earthy Jerusalem where Jesus was crucified. What the appropriately named Trash desires therein is not rest and peace, but rather shrieks, rapes, subjugations, and a "Great Burning"—"Cities going up like bombs. Cultivated fields drawn in line of fire."

AN ALL-AMERICAN ANTICHRIST

While the figures of Lloyd and Trash might be the right and left sides of Flagg's demonic kingdom, more interesting are the pseudorational and often mutually contradictory manifestations of Flagg in American culture. Pockets in his "faded pegged jeans" were filled with "fifty different kinds" of "literature"—the "dangers of atomic power plants, the role played by the International Jewish Cartel in the overthrow of friendly governments, the CIA, the farm workers' union, the Jehovah's Witnesses . . . the Blacks for Militant Equality, the Kode of the Klan." When Flagg, called by one of the characters (Glen Bateman) the "last magician of rational thought," walked into a meeting, the backbiting, recriminations, and accusations would cease. Mysteriously, he brought to these meetings "some old and terrible engine of destruction," something a "thousand times worse than the plastic explosive made in the basement labs of renegade chemistry students or the black market arms obtained from some greedy army post supply sergeant"—a "device gone rusty with blood, but now ready again," carried to the meeting in which he intrudes like "some infernal gift." King observes that when the discussion that had been "hysterical babble" and "ideological rhetoric" began again, everything would surprisingly be "rational and disciplined—as rational and disciplined as madmen can make it, and things would be agreed upon." In such a manner, the ubiquitous "Antichrist" infiltrated a "hundred different Committees of Responsibility." He participated in the civil rights marches of 1960 and 1961 and churches "exploded as if some miracle inside them had grown too big to be contained." Not unexpectedly, he encountered a certain Mr. Oswald [the assassin of President Kennedy], who was handing out tracts urging America to leave Cuba alone. Possessed of a "fiery grin," he terrified mothers who, seeing him, quickly used to "grab up their children and pull them into the house."

"Baby, Can You Dig Your Man?"

"Baby, Can You Dig Your Man?" is the repeated line in the rock song that makes singer-composer Larry Underwood wealthy and famous, a line that is repeated so often in the beginning of *The Stand* that it becomes a kind of motif, acquiring various layers of implication as the plot unfolds. The account of the creation and popularization of Larry's man-digging song in chapter 5 is preceded by the quarrel between Franny Goldsmith and her boy friend Jess Rider over Fran's unexpected pregnancy, and by the accidental escape of deadly flu viruses from the western California experimental laboratory. The question—"Can you dig your man?"—has one meaning (almost comical) in the context of the copulative carelessness that resulted in Fran's seemingly unfortunate pregnancy. In a mocking dialogue with her lover (Jess), the begetter of her unwanted child, she cleverly lists the possible errors that might account for her present condition: "Well, what I figure is *one*, somebody in the quality control department of the jolly old Orvil factory [manufacturer of birth control devices] was asleep at the switch when my batch of pills went by on the conveyor belt, or *two*, they are feeding you guys something in the UNH messhall that builds up sperm, or *three*, I forgot to take a pill and have since forgotten I forgot."

The six-word man-digging question has yet another implication, quite bitter and sardonic, when scientist Billy Starkey conducts an imaginary conversation with his daughter (Cindy Hammer) to inform her of the sudden death of her young husband, whose ironical nickname is "Vic" (i.e., "Victory"). Starkey tries to explain the scientific mistake:

> You see, there was a goof. Somebody made a mistake with a box. Somebody else forgot to pull a switch that would have sealed off the base. The lag was only twenty-three seconds, but it was enough. . . . The boxes were put together by female technicians, and they're put together circuit by circuit so none of them really know what they're doing. One of them was maybe thinking about what to make for supper, and whoever was supposed to check her work was maybe thinking about trading the family car.

The accidental and fatal release of the experimental superflu virus (that produces death so universal as to turn the earth into a virtual crypt) is thus counterbalanced—and eventually counteracted—by the accidental impregnation of Franny Goldsmith (that will produce a child who will possess the biological power to "wear down" the virulence of the superflu and conquer it). This child, like the child of the headless woman in [King's novella] "Breathing Method," will be born within the twelve-day Christmas season (4 January 1986), drawing a somewhat imperfect yet obviously intentional analogy with the Christ child. The nickname of the child's father is "Jess," an abbreviated form of Jesse, the father of David in the Old Testament (1 Samuel 16). The child's ability to resist is the "stand" he makes against Captain Trips for several days after his birth—hence the name of book 3, "The Stand" (dated 7 September 1985–10 January 1986), and the name of the novel itself.

A HELLISH MARRIAGE

Of the various sexual encounters throughout the novel, the most searing is the "infernal marriage" between Randall Flagg and Nadine Cross, who has been saving herself for "something special." Nadine's inability to endure the cold phallic advances of Randall, although she has long been waiting for them, add layer upon layer of horror to the rock theme, "Baby, can you dig your man?" In bedding down Nadine and Randall in the context of repellant images, *The Stand* befouls sexuality by imagining its ultimate horror: a "caked and long-hidden lust," an "ageless pimple . . . about to spew forth some noisome fluid," "something terrible . . . beating with a life of its own beneath the notched coldness of his zipper." Copulation with Flagg is made as terrifying and forbidding as a descent into the ultimate ice-lake, the Cocytus, which forms the ninth and last circle of Dante's hell. One is reminded of what, earlier, Abigail Trotts said to Nadine Cross: "When you get there, you'll find out that hell is cold":

> And when the dead coldness of him slipped into her the shriek ripped up and out of her, bolted free, and she struggled, and the struggle was useless. He battered into her, invader, destroyer, and the cold blood gushed down her thighs . . . and the moon was in her eyes, cold and silver fire, and when he came it was like molten iron, molten *pig* iron, molten *brass*, and she came herself, came in screaming, incredible pleasure, came in terror, in horror, passing through the pig iron and brass gates into the desert land of insanity. . . .

It is not unusual for King to expand upon earlier myths, poems, legends, and fairy tales. Here he zeroes into a missing aspect of [poet William Butler] Yeats's "The Second Coming." He seems also to have in mind the sexual encounter of the swan (actually Zeus) and the mother of Helen in what Yeats considered an important companion piece, "Leda and the Swan," especially the lines: "a shudder in the loins engenders there / A broken wall, and Agamemnon dead." Unlike the Leda poem, however, "The Second Coming" does not actualize the genital contact between the parents of the

Antichrist, observing only that the "beast" "slouches to Beth-lehem to be born." What Yeats lacks, King here supplies: the sexual action. The Yeats poem (the name mispronounced "Yeets") is actually dwelt upon at some length by scientist Billy Starkey in one of the earlier sections of *The Stand*, when he quotes a few significant lines, but especially emphasizes that the "rough beast [i.e., "Captain Trips"] is on his way."

POWERFUL MOMENTS

Though much of *The Stand* is disjointed and needlessly rambling—perhaps, carrying out the twentieth-century Yeats theme of "The Second Coming" that "things fall apart" because "center cannot hold"—there are genuine moments of imaginative power, such as this bestial conjoining of those two abominations, Flagg and Cross, whose names with their perverted patriotic and religious connotations have by no means been randomly selected. Caught in the apocalypse of A6, the despairing scientist, Billy Starkey, is attempting to "dig" his man, that is, attempting to understand the prophetical Irish poet William Butler Yeats.

Ultimately, however, the true "baby" who can "dig" (i.e., "bury") his man ("Captain Trips") is none other than Fran's illegitimate child, baby Peter, the son of Jess, whose name has both religious and Freudian connotations. Peter is the world's only hope. However, having made his "stand" as a baby against Captain Trips, Peter should, when he grows up, try to make yet another "stand" by reminding his own children that the "*toys are death*," "*flashburns*," "*radiation sickness and black choking plague*." In his own strange way—and perhaps quite unconsciously—Stephen King is developing his "baby" from an historical incident: a cryptic telegram, addressed to Secretary of War Henry Stimson at the Potsdam conference in July 1945, referring to the atomic bomb about to be dropped on Hiroshima as a husky "Little Boy" that has just been delivered.

Developing an anti-Christian image from William Blake's

famous poem "The Tiger," a grown-up Peter will eventually be able to warn future generations that some Lovecraftian *"devil in men's hands guided the hands of God when they were made"*—what Winston Churchill called, upon learning of the atomic bomb for the first time at Potsdam, the "Second Coming in wrath." Peter's final admonition is that *"this empty world"* should be the future world's *"copybook,"* the copybook being, no doubt, King's eight-hundred-page *Stand.* Though this lengthy novel has brilliant subsections— little vignettes like the tender biography of deaf-and-dumb Nick Andros in chapter 13—the novel as a whole tends to be tedious. In attempting an American epic to rival Tolstoy's *War and Peace,* Dostoevski's *Brothers Karamazov,* Melville's *Moby-Dick,* and Mitchell's *Gone with the Wind,* King ended up producing in *The Stand* a pseudophilosophic speculation on Antichrist and the Apocalypse. Small wonder to find the author acknowledging that, during the composition of *The Stand,* he "actively hated the book" and considered it his "own little Viet-Nam."

Like a miniature atom bomb, the eight-page short story "Night Surf" packs a far more powerful wallop than *The Stand* without bothering the reader with—desirable as they might be in the real world—tedious ramblings about democracy and the reestablishment of the Constitution. One of the ironies of the current taste in popular fiction is that whereas *The Stand* is extremely interesting to young readers (consistently described as their favorite among Stephen King's novels), the more brilliantly crafted "Night Surf" (based on precisely the same theme) does not seem to attract similar youthful enthusiasm. Unlike the expansive *Stand,* an extravagant apocalyptic fantasy, "Night Surf" perhaps moves—in a context of rock music and the drug cult—too quickly and too close to the uncomfortable truth of universal selfishness and indifference to the sufferings of others.

Donna Trenton: A Modern American Heroine

Carol A. Senf

In *Cujo*, Donna Trenton and her young son are trapped inside their car by a vicious, rabid dog. Published in 1981, the book was King's first full-length novel to forgo supernatural elements of horror in favor of the psychological terror that Donna undergoes as she fights to save herself and her child. Donna ultimately fends off the dog only to discover that her son has died of seizures. *Cujo* comes, for many readers, to an almost unbearably sad conclusion.

But as Carol A. Senf points out in the following selection, Donna Trenton's survival of the ordeal, however marred by her son's death, represents a victory over the stifling constraints of her middle-class marriage and family values (favorite targets of King's satire). Donna's entrapment in her inexpensive Pinto serves, according to Senf, as a metaphor for her entrapment in her marriage. Even the qualitative difference between the two cars—her husband's vehicle is a luxurious Jaguar, hers an inexpensive "family" automobile—underscores the unequal partnership of the Trenton union. Senf argues that the heroine's courage and resourcefulness are an affirmative portrait of the late-twentieth-century American woman's fight against oppressive social norms: the inequality of marital roles, the emptiness of material comforts, and the stereotype of female helplessness that persisted despite the gains of the 1960s women's movement. Literally trapped in a situation beyond her control, Donna manages through courage and force of will to prevail, although her ultimate victory is bittersweet. To this extent, Donna is a precursor to the gutsy heroines who overcome abuse in later King novels such as *Gerald's Game, Dolores Claiborne,* and *Rose Madder.*

Carol A. Senf, an associate professor of Georgia Institute of Technology's School of Literature, Communication, and Culture, is author of *The Vampire in Nineteenth Century Literature* (1988) and *Dracula: Between Tradition and Modernism* (1998).

[Since the late 1970s] Stephen King has been an enormously popular writer, and part of the reason for that popularity is the fact that his books feature ordinary human characters with whom the reader can readily identify. Moreover these ordinary people become heroes and heroines because they confront unspeakable horrors with courage and conviction.

By far the strongest of King's heroines is Donna Trenton in *Cujo.* To establish her as a modern American heroine, King does two things: First he places her in a realistic environment and shows her confronting the same problems that face ordinary human beings today; second he deliberately contrasts her with the dependent women of earlier Gothic literature and horror films, the women her son Tad thinks of when he dreams of warning her about the monster in his closet: "*Be careful, Mommy, they* [monsters] *eat the ladies! In all the movies they catch the ladies and carry them off and eat them!*" Though Tad never confesses his fears to his mother, Donna is aware of the tradition of female weakness and passivity. A former librarian, she repeatedly compares herself—sometimes facetiously but more often seriously—to a damsel in distress and her husband to the knight who will rescue her. In fact, King reveals that Donna must abandon the notion that the heroine is someone to be rescued. Only then can she attempt to save both her son and herself from the rabid Cujo, a monster that King emphasizes is a symbol for all the evil forces against which human beings must struggle, only then can she become a suitable representative of the modern, more assertive woman.

In a similar fashion, Charity Camber [another character in

Cujo], a working class version of the trapped American woman, accepts responsibility for herself and her son and escapes from a brutal and abusive husband. A lesser version of the heroine, Charity is also a strong and courageous woman with whom twentieth-century readers can be proud to identify.

KING'S INTEREST IN ORDINARY LIVES

Although King is often identified as a writer of supernatural horror because of his early novels, *Salem's Lot* and *The Shining*, his emphasis on ordinary human life is clear from the very beginning of *Cujo*, which he prefaces with the following quotation from [poet] W.H. Auden's "Musee des Beaux Arts":

> About suffering they were never wrong,
> The Old Masters: how well they understood
> Its human position; how it takes place
> While someone else is eating or opening a window or just
>   walking dully along . . .

By choosing this quotation, King emphasizes the human rather than the superhuman; and he distances himself still further from his early novels in the rest of *Cujo*. Reinforcing the ordinary quality of human suffering is the first page of the novel, which identifies the monster in Castle Rock, Maine, as a sick human being:

> He was not werewolf, vampire, ghoul, or unnameable
> creature from the enchanted forest or from the snowy
> wastes; he was only a cop named Frank Dodd with men-
> tal and sexual problems.

King is obviously playing with the readers' expectations. However, the figure of Frank Dodd, a sick and destructive human being rather than a vampire or a haunted house, will appear again and again in the novel, sometimes linked with Cujo, another example of an evil that occurs within the natural world:

> Screaming, he got both hands under the dog's muzzle

> again and yanked it up. For a moment, staring into
> those dark, crazed eyes . . . he thought: *Hello, Frank. It's
> you, isn't it? Was hell too hot for you?*

Despite Sheriff Bannerman's reference to Dodd's return from
the grave, however, King expects the reader to recognize that
Cujo and Dodd are both examples of evil within the natural
world, not supernatural Evil.

THE PLIGHT OF MODERN AMERICAN WOMEN IN *CUJO*

In addition to being about natural evil, *Cujo* is about
women. Although Bannerman, Joe Camber, and Gary Pervier are men victims of Cujo and Vic Trenton is practically
destroyed by the death of his son, *Cujo*—more than King's
other novels (with the possible exception of *Carrie*) focuses
on women's experiences, From the first paragraph, which
catalogues Frank Dodd's six victims—all women or young
girls—to the last, the novel scrutinizes the lives of women in
twentieth-century America. . . .

Aware of male fears of women, King is able to use this understanding in his books. Carrie's extraordinary power is un-
leashed in one terrifying night that destroys an entire town,
but *Cujo* reveals that women terrify men even with less extraordinary strength. Arriving on the scene after his wife has
finally overcome Cujo, Vic Trenton wants to escape rather
than offer her comfort for her ordeal:

> He didn't know what he had expected, but it hadn't been
> this. He had been afraid, but the sight of his wife . . .
> standing over the twisted and smashed thing in the
> driveway, striking it again and again with something
> that looked like a caveman's club . . . that turned his fear
> to a bright, silvery panic. . . . For one infinite moment,
> which he would never admit to himself later, he felt an
> impulse to throw the Jag in reverse and drive away . . .
> to drive forever. What was going on in this still and
> sunny door yard was monstrous.

Especially perceptive here are King's recognition that men

rarely admit their fear of women openly and his use of the word "monstrous" to describe one man's response to a woman's exhibition of power. He knows that such exhibits are so rare that they inspire awe and terror.

PARALLEL WIVES IN *CUJO*

Although *Cujo* culminates with Donna's horrifying ordeal and her need for exceptional courage, most of the novel takes place within the minds of Donna and Charity as they face more ordinary problems. Douglas Winter observes of the novel that its "storyline evolves about two marriages," and that both of these "marriages are in jeopardy."

Of the two Charity is less interesting, and King spends less time on her because her problems are less psychologically complex. This is not to say that her problems are not serious—in some ways more serious than Donna's—for Charity is married to a physically abusive man:

> Joe had used his hands on her a few times in the course of their marriage, and she had learned. . . . Now she did what Joe told her and rarely argued. She guessed Brett was that way too. But she feared for the boy sometimes.

Most of the sections that involve Charity focus on her attempts to show her son a better way of life, one that is physically very different from their life with Joe. Escaping even briefly from Joe requires both luck and skill—the good luck of winning the lottery and skill in the courage to approach her husband. In fact, King reveals that she could "sometimes gain the upper hand just by seeming brave. Not always, but sometimes." King also lets the reader know that these moments of bravery are risky, however, for the Camber marriage, like so many other marriages, is essentially unequal: "Joe could go places alone or with his friends, but she couldn't, not even with Brett in tow. That was one of their marriage's ground rules."

Joe's power over Charity stems both from his greater physical strength and from the economic advantage of having money to spend as he chooses. Probing Charity's mind after she wins the lottery, King reveals to the reader how economic dependence on their husbands affects women:

> Lady Luck had singled her out. For the first time in her life, maybe for the only time, that heavy muslin drape of the everyday had been twitched a little, showing her a bright and shining world beyond. She was a practical woman, and in her heart she knew that she hated her husband more than a little, but that they would grow old together, and he would die, leaving her with his debts and . . . perhaps with his spoilt son.

In short, five thousand dollars isn't enough to provide her and Brett with more than a brief escape.

If King had stopped his portrait here, the reader would be left with a kind of caricature of an unliberated woman who is trapped by economic dependence and fear of physical power. However, King recognizes that many women are not able to take charge of their lives because they are also trapped by powerful internal compulsions, in Charity's case by love for the man who continues to victimize her:

> Was she going to kid herself and say that she did not, even now, in some way love the man she had married? That she stayed with him only out of duty, or for the sake of the child (*that* was a bitter laugh; if she ever left him it would be for the sake of the child)? . . . That he could not, sometimes at the most unexpected moments . . . be tender.

Passages like this one focus on the kinds of complex emotional issues that King's ordinary characters face every day and negate a criticism so often leveled against popular writers like King—that they create nothing but caricatures. Moreover, it negates [critic] Chelsea Quinn Yarbro's specific criticism that King cannot "develop a believable woman character between the ages of seventeen and sixty." Both

Donna and Charity are believable human beings because they confront the ordinary problems faced by the readers. The character of Charity, however, is more clearly modeled on an older notion of the heroine as a person to be rescued by someone else, by circumstance, or by luck. Less heroic than Donna, Charity escapes from her husband largely because of luck rather than because of skill and self knowledge. Nonetheless, at the end of the novel, she is a confident and independent woman who is working to achieve her own goals. Such independence and preparation for her son's college education could not have happened while she was married to Joe Camber.

If Charity is believable, strong, and almost heroic, Donna is an ordinary woman who becomes the modern American heroine. Middle class and college educated—a librarian married to an advertising executive—Donna is also much more articulate about her condition as a woman and about everything that being a woman means.

INEQUALITY IN THE TRENTON MARRIAGE

Despite these differences, King very carefully highlights significant similarities in the two women. The first of these similarities is the fact that Donna, like Charity, is aware of her physical limitations. Although Donna is a large woman—five-eleven and "an inch taller than Vic when she wore heels"—and an athlete, she is easily physically intimidated by both Steve Kemp and Joe Camber; and King's careful relating of Donna's thoughts also reminds us of how women are—more often than men—influenced by their physical condition:

> Falling off the back porch when she was five and breaking her wrist.

> Looking down at herself . . . when she was a high school freshman and seeing to her utter shame and horror that there were spots of blood on her light blue linen skirt.

> . . . Holding Tad in her arms, newborn, then the nurse
> taking him away; she wanted to tell the nurse not to do
> that . . . but she was too weak to talk. . . .

Furthermore, though her husband is not the kind of man to employ physical force, King makes it clear that Vic is in control, for Donna "hadn't wanted to come to Maine and had been appalled when Vic had sprung the idea on her." Such details suggest that the Trenton marriage is unequal and that Vic makes the important decisions.

King, who is exceptionally sensitive to material culture in the twentieth century, further reveals the inequality in their marriage by focusing on the cars they drive, an emphasis that clearly reveals Donna's economic dependence. Vic drives an expensive imported sports car, a Jaguar, while Donna drives one of the least expensive automobiles ever produced in Detroit, the Ford Pinto. In this way King reveals that Vic is a man who likes to pamper himself; and, when he shows that Vic is totally aware of the media attention to the dangers associated with driving the Pinto, he also reveals that such pampering may be at the expense of his family. Ironically, however, Donna and Tad don't die inside a burning Pinto. Donna survives, and Tad dies of dehydration when Cujo traps them inside the Pinto during three of the hottest days of the year.

Furthermore, like Charity Camber, Donna feels trapped though her feelings of entrapment are only partially due to lack of money. A former professional, Donna contemplates going back to work. However, she ultimately labels it a "ridiculous notion, and she shelved it after running some figures on her pocket calculator." Here—as elsewhere—King uses financial worries to emphasize ordinary problems, the kind of problems a reader might face. However, despite the reference to money here and elsewhere in the novel—Vic's new advertising agency is having financial difficulty, for example—Donna's problems are not lack of money, but the fact that she has too much time on her hands—time to worry about her loss of identity. Donna recognizes the problem:

She started to sharpshoot at Vic about little things, sublimating the big things because they were hard to define and even harder to articulate. Things like loss and fear and getting older. Things like being lonely and then getting terrified of being lonely. . . . Feeling jealous because his life was a daily struggle to build something . . . and her life was back here, getting Tad through the day.

DONNA'S CRISIS AND QUEST FOR CONTROL

Donna's later heroism is foreshadowed when King shows that she can't escape the loneliness in the ways that are acceptable for women: volunteer work, "hen parties," and soap operas. A doer and a confronter rather than an escapist, Donna tries to fill her life in traditionally acceptable ways—through housework and through caring for her son. She realizes, however, that this work won't last because "every year the world gets another little slice of him." Ultimately her loneliness and sense of frustration lead her to a disastrous affair with Steve Kemp, a man as physically brutal as Joe Camber and certainly more psychologically abusive.

The affair with Kemp is an illustration of Donna's weakness—of her tendency to drift until someone else provides her with a solution. On the other hand, the scene in which she ends the affair even though he threatens to rape her in her own kitchen foreshadows the final climactic scene when she decides that she cannot depend on someone else:

> She had been afraid to use her loudest voice, and had done so only when it became absolutely necessary. Because that was where civilization came to an abrupt, screeching halt. That was the place where the tar turned to dirt. If they wouldn't listen when you used your very loudest voice, a scream became your only recourse.

Ironically, although Donna fears the absence of civilization, she will discover herself only when she has rid herself of civilization and its expectations for women. Screaming at

Kemp, she discovers her power over him: "And if I get a chance to tear your balls off or put one of your eyes out, I won't hesitate." It is a power that women rarely achieve.

Trapped by Cujo in the Pinto, which becomes a symbol of her entire life as a dependent, Donna slowly begins to take control of her life. At first, clearly expecting to be rescued—by Vic, by the mailman when he comes to the Cambers, by anyone—she remains like the old style passive heroine:

> She didn't know why no one had answered the SOS she had been beeping out. In a book, someone would have come. It was the heroine's reward for having thought up such a clever idea. But no one had come.

Alone in the Pinto, with only her four-year-old son for company, Donna becomes a new kind of heroine, a woman who takes control of her life rather than waiting for someone—the proverbial knight—to save her. In fact, Donna begins to realize during the ordeal that she is a new kind of woman:

> That had been the first time she had really believed—believed in her gut—that she was going to grow up and become a woman, a woman with at least a fighting chance to be a *better* woman than her own mother, who could get into such a frightening state over what was really such a little thing. . . .

Finally, forced again by external circumstances to take matters into her own hands, Donna contrasts herself to the heroines of earlier literature, the traditional damsels in distress:

> The time had come, and Donna knew it. . . . No one was going to come. There was going to be no knight on a silver steed riding up Town Road No. 3—Travis McGee was apparently otherwise engaged.
>
> Tad was dying.

Reminding the reader again that *Cujo* takes place in the real world, King has Donna's victory over Cujo come too late to save Tad. The little boy dies while his mother is battling the monster; and Donna, who had earlier saved his life when his tongue blocks his windpipe and who finally overcomes the monstrous dog, cannot bring him back to life. It is thus a hollow victory. Her marriage in jeopardy and her son dead, Donna has lost all the things that supposedly provided meaning for traditional heroines. Realizing, however, that the modern heroine must not be afraid to confront life, readers should feel purged by their vicarious participation in her victory. As Donna herself recognizes before she leaves to do battle, this ability to confront one's problems is all that matters:

> Had this terrible vigil been only a matter of hours, or had it been her whole life? Surely everything that had gone before had been a dream, little more than a short wait in the wings? The mother who had seemed to be disgusted and repulsed by all those around her, the well-meaning but ineffectual father, the schools, the friends, the dates and dances—they were all a dream to her now. . . . Nothing mattered, nothing *was* but this silent and sunstruck dooryard where death had been dealt and yet more death waited in the cards. . . . The old monster kept his watch still. . . .

King seems to realize here that his readers—especially his women readers—are ready for a new kind of heroine, a woman who is prepared to leave behind triviality—the constant dusting of pottery knickknacks that Donna equates with women's lives—and confront the unspeakable with courage and conviction.

THE IMPORTANCE OF READER IDENTIFICATION

Recognizing his readers' needs, Stephen King makes Donna Trenton a new kind of heroine. First, he presents her as an ordinary human being, one troubled by the same kinds of problems that confront ordinary human beings, and he shows that such an ordinary human being can live with dignity and courage. Finally he has this ordinary person confront an exceptional—almost superhuman—adversary.

Stephen King has become an immensely popular writer, and part of that popularity is undoubtedly his ability to write a suspenseful story. However, another—and probably more important—reason for his popularity stems from his ability to create characters with whom the readers can readily identify. Although most of his novels focus on men characters, *Cujo* scrutinizes the problems that confront twentieth-century American women. Donna and Charity are ordinary women, one middle class, well educated and articulate; the other, working class, uneducated, and less introspective. Despite seemingly overwhelming odds, each woman manages to take control of her life. Donna especially in her display of courage becomes a new American heroine, a strong woman with whom women in the twentieth century can be proud to identify.

Adolescent Angst in *Rage*

Michael R. Collings

Critical and popular interest in *Rage*, one of King's early short novels published under the pseudonym Richard Bachman in 1977 soared in the aftermath of a spate of school shootings in the 1990s, in which at least one adolescent shooter claimed to have been inspired by the work. King himself was so concerned that his story of teen alienation might be influencing troubled teens to imitate the actions of his young protagonist Charlie, who shoots a teacher and holds his classmates hostage, that he addressed the matter in a preface to a later edition of *Rage*. He cautioned young readers to express their own anger and frustration as he did in writing a story rather than acting on their emotions. King ultimately asked his publisher to cease reissuing the novel.

Michael R. Collings, author of the following selection, is an academic critic who has published extensively on King, including several books. His commentary describes *Rage*'s origins and publication and assesses its status in the King canon. For Collings, *Rage* is clearly a juvenile work that in some ways is dated by its 1960s social psychology. However, the short novel's insight into adolescent rebellion against adult authority mark *Rage* as an interesting early endeavor. Professor Michael R. Collings currently directs the creative writing program at Pepperdine University.

King's fourth published novel represents one of his earliest attempts at full-length narrative. One of five novel manuscripts completed before King wrote *Carrie, Rage* was begun in 1966 under the title *Getting It On*, when King was a senior in high

Michael R. Collings, "*Rage* (1977)," *The Stephen King Companion*, revised edition, edited by George Beahm. Kansas City, MO: Andrews McMeel, 1995. Copyright © 1995 by George and Mary Beahm. Reproduced by permission.

school. Left unfinished for several years, it was completed in 1971 and published six years later when, as King says in the introduction to *The Bachman Books*, it "occurred to [him] that [he] ought to publish *Getting It On* . . . which Double-day *almost* published two years before they published *Carrie*."

Had the novel been published under King's name in 1977, following the increasing maturity and complexity of *Carrie, 'Salem's Lot,* and *The Shining*, it might well have been seen as a disappointment by his growing numbers of fans—by March 1977, all three novels had appeared on the best-seller lists, with *The Shining* marking King's hardcover debut. It seems unlikely that at that time even the coattails of King's name would have been sufficient to propel *Rage* to best-seller status; a solid work, it is also far more restricted in scope, in characterization, in theme, and in achievement than the first three "King" novels, as is to be expected from what is essentially juvenilia.

As a "Richard Bachman" novel, however, *Rage* was forced to make its own way; and until King's public acknowledgment of his pseudonym in February 1985 and the near hysteria that erupted among segments of King's reading public, the novel was not subjected to comparison to King's later, more sophisticated works. That is perhaps as it should be. The Bachman novels are, in general, unlike most of the works published under King's own name—tauter in structure, less dependent upon external horrors, more closely connected to mainstream fiction . . . or at least the illusion of "reality" propounded by mainstream fiction.

A STUDY IN TEEN ANGST

Rage is an extended study in adolescent *angst*, beginning with its first-person killer/protagonist, Charlie Dekker, and spreading like an infection throughout the high school class he holds hostage. The action is direct and brutal: Dekker meets with the principal for disciplinary action after Dekker nearly killed the shop teacher. He is expelled and told to leave school immediately. He stops at his locker, takes out a pistol, returns to class, shoots the teacher and intimidates the students until it is too late for them to escape. For the next several hours, he invites them to "get it on" with him—to examine their own lives and motives, their frustrations and fears. After systematically making fools of school and police officials. Charlie lets the class go and fakes the police into shooting him.

Oh, and along the way, he just as systematically destroys the mind of the one student who represents the adults idealized view of normal childhood and does so with the active aid of everyone else in the class.

PARENTS AND CHILDREN

The novel is not based on action, as King himself recognizes, but on psychology and penetration, primarily into the illusions held by adults about their roles in parenting and educating children, and the illusions held by children about their roles as subordinates to their parents. By placing his story of childhood memories revisited, examined, and finally exorcised (by some of the students, at least) among a classroom full of high school seniors about to be thrust into adult responsibility whether they like it or not, King provides an ideal fulcrum for assessing the deficiencies of parenting and socialization. Charlie Dekker is not the only member of the class tottering on the edge of sanity, and he is not the only one to tip the balance during the course of the novel.

FLAWS AND STRENGTHS

There are weaknesses in the novel. It is preachy. It presupposes certain 1960s Freudian truisms that are less rigidly accepted today. It reduces adults to hollow, posturing fools incapable of dealing with Charlie's manic cleverness. It breaks its own narrative mode at the conclusion with the intrusion of court documents, memos, and letters of the same sort that strengthened *Carrie;* here they seem almost anticlimactic.

The first-person narrative places a greater burden on Charlie Dekker than he is able to bear, since at times he seems more abstract image of rebellious teen than concrete person.

On the other hand, there are also strengths, many paradoxically growing out of the weaknesses. Charlie's obsession with his own interior processes gives him the momentary authority to set the entire class-sized encounter session in progress and to draw the darkest secrets from each of his classmates. And more than the horror of Charlie's murders, more than the terror of being in a locked classroom with a killer, more than watching the adult world stand by, bumbling and helpless, those secrets define the purging effects of "getting it on" for characters willing to reach inside, reveal the darkness, and accept it.

Compared with *It*, *The Stand*, or *The Shining*, *Rage* is certainly a weaker novel and a lesser achievement. On its own terms, however, with its narrowly defined characters, perhaps the most limited time span of any King novel or story, strictly focused themes and development, and idiosyncratic narrative voice, it nevertheless manages to hold its own as a document of a past time and as a novel examining ongoing human crises and resolutions.

The Vampire Tradition in *Misery*

Natalie Schroeder

Stephen King's popularity was largely responsible for a great revival, even renaissance, of popular horror fiction. In the 1980s and 1990s, writers such as Dean Koontz, Robert McCammon, John Saul, and Anne Rice joined King as regulars on hardcover best-seller lists. Vampire novels in particular proliferated, from Rice's hugely successful *Vampire Chronicles* to quirkier contributions by Brian Lumley and Poppy Z. Brite. Yet with the exceptions of his second novel *'Salem's Lot* and the short story "The Night Flyer," King has largely avoided the vampire subgenre, a fact that may be due to either its quasierotic qualities (about which King admits a degree of squeamishness) or its near-cliché status in contemporary horror writing. Nonetheless, Natalie Schroeder argues in the following selection that *Misery*, one of King's nonsupernatural works, may be read as a naturalistic vampire novel, with main character Annie as the predatory, blood-sucking monster.

Natalie Schroeder, an associate professor of English at the University of Mississippi, has published extensively on Victorian literature, popular literature, and feminism.

Paul Sheldon, the kidnapped protagonist of Stephen King's *Misery*, echoes his creator when he discusses his incredible financial success and his own special talents as a writer: "there are lots of guys out there who write a better prose line than I do and who have a better understanding of what people are really like and what humanity is supposed to mean—. But if

Natalie Schroeder, "Stephen King's *Misery:* Freudian Sexual Symbolism and the Battle of the Sexes," *Journal of Popular Culture*, vol. 30, Fall 1996, pp. 137–48.

you want me to take you away, to scare you or involve you or make you cry or grin, yea, I can. I can bring it to you and keep bringing it until you holler uncle. I am able. I CAN."

Don Herron, in fact, attributes King's success as a best-selling novelist to his use of horror, which is "firmly based in the material world": "Horror springs in King's stories from contemporary social *reality*, and I'd say it is this quality more than any other that has made King a bestseller. King doesn't take vampires seriously, but you would have to be a fool or a saint not to recognize and react to the pervasive horror in everyday life." Such horror is what [Sigmund] Freud calls "The Uncanny"—"that class of terrifying which leads back to something long known to us, very familiar," which has been repressed.

[Gary] Hoppenstand and [Ray B.] Browne call *Misery*, King's eighteenth novel, "a thinly veiled self-examination of his fans, his writing, and his genre work." But *Misery* is also a psychological horror story without the supernatural—a frightening tale of the reality of everyday life, of repressed fears, of pain, frustration, loneliness, insecurity, insanity, dependence, and disintegration. And although there are no explicit sexual scenes in the novel, *Misery* exploits Freudian metaphorical representations of sexuality. In *Danse Macabre*, in fact, King states that "sex continues to be a driving force in the horror genre sometimes presented in disguised Freudian terms . . . [and] much of the sex . . . is deeply involved in power tripping; it's sex based on relationships where one partner is largely under control of the other; sex which inevitably leads to some bad end." *Misery* depicts an ultra-violent sexual battle which ends in a stalemate.

King also discusses the strong sexual undertones in vampire fiction. Much of the evil of Bram Stoker's Count Dracula, he says, "is a perverse sexual evil," while Renfield symbolizes the root source of vampirism—cannibalism. King equates the bite of the vampire (male and female) with oral rape. And because readers have fears of pending disaster, of their own mortality, and of their sexual potency, King, like Paul Sheldon, scares and involves his readers.

ANNIE'S MONSTROUS FEMININITY

At the beginning of *Misery*, Paul Sheldon regains consciousness to learn gradually that he is the victim of a car wreck and that he has been saved and imprisoned by Annie Wilkes, a middle-aged, manic-depressive ex-nurse who is his most avid fan. King's first description of her establishes her as androgynous—a phallic woman: "She was a big woman who, other than the large but unwelcoming swell of her bosom under the gray cardigan sweater she always wore, seemed to have no feminine curves at all—There was no defined roundness of hip or buttock or even calf below the endless succession of wool skirts she wore in the house (she retired to her unseen room to put on jeans before doing her outside chores). Her body was big but not generous. There was a feeling about her of clots and roadblocks rather than welcoming orifices or even open spaces, areas of hiatus."

Locked in a room in Annie's isolated farmhouse overlooking a mountainous terrain, Paul becomes an ironic version of Misery, the persecuted heroine of his own Gothic romance series. Annie, a dowdy, unexotic villain who becomes the Bourka Bee-Goddess of Sheldon's newest novel, almost succeeds in consuming him. She drains him of his essential self and scrapes away "the liver and lights of his spirit."

VAMPIRE IMAGERY

Like a vampire, Annie Wilkes is an oral rapist. Artificial respiration in *Misery* is metaphoric of both rebirth and undeath (through a vampire's bite), and Paul awakens to pain, stink, and infection: "When the lips were pulled back he smelled his warder for the first time, smelled her on the outrush of the breath she had forced into him the way a man might force a part of himself into an unwilling woman, a dreadful mixed stench of vanilla cookies and chocolate ice cream and chicken gravy and peanut-butter fudge." Annie's gluttony is juxtaposed to the figurative violation of his body: before he has a chance to start breathing, she "rape[s] him full of her air again." King extends the vampire metaphor later when Annie squeezes the rat she caught in her trap, crushes its bones, and sucks its blood from her fingers. Left alone with no food, Paul looks at the mangled rat and laughs hysterically: "'Who *said* she didn't leave me anything to eat?' he asked the room, and laughed even harder. In the empty house, Paul Sheldon's Laughing Place sounded like the padded cell of a madman." Like a vampire's victim, Paul is now undead—a metaphorical vampire himself.

Vampire imagery reappears when Annie kills the state trooper. She stabs him with the cross she had placed on her dead cow's grave; when she pulls the cross free, its sharpened point breaks off, "leaving a jagged splintering stump." As she drives the stump into the trooper's back, buttocks, upper thigh, neck, and crotch, she appears to Paul "like a woman trying to kill a vampire." The cross is also a phallic symbol. The murder is another figurative rape, in which Annie wins a power struggle with a male figure of authority. To Paul, she has "*become* a goddess, a thing that was half woman and half Lawnboy, a weird female centaur."

SEXUAL CAPTIVITY AND COERCION

The sexual undertones noted above are among many throughout the novel. After Paul regains his will to live, for example, Annie makes him her prostitute by forcing him to write a new Misery-novel: "I was driving to the West Coast to celebrate my liberation from the state of whoredom," he thinks. "What you did was to pull me out of the wreck when I crashed my car and stick me back in the crib again. Two dollar straight up, four dollar I take you aroun the worl [sic]." The used Royal typewriter with the missing "n" becomes a symbol of his prostitution; and King punctuates this relationship when Annie self-righteously comments that Ms.

Dartmonger, the woman who sold her the typewriter, ought to be named Whoremonger because she has been married twice and is now living with a bartender. Annie casually ignores the fact that she is a divorcee, that she and her last victim, Andrew Pomeroy, were lovers, and that she is also living with a man. As Annie's whore, Paul is forced to endure repulsive embraces, words of endearment, and tender melting looks. After he lends her the money to pay her taxes, for example, she treats him with tenderness: "Her own eyes glistened as she leaned forward and gently touched his lips. He smelled something on her breath, something from the dark and sour chambers inside her, something that smelled like dead fish. . . . His stomach clenched, but he smiled at her. 'I love you, dear,' she said."

The sexual undertones are not limited to rape and prostitution; they also reverberate of incest. Annie becomes not only Paul's wife/lover, but also his mother. When Paul first regains consciousness, he reverts to his childhood. He is Paulie with his mother and father at Revere Beach, watching the pilings appear between the waves. He has regressed to the stage of infant orality as he greedily sucks his medication from Annie's fingers: "She brought him two every six hours, first announcing her presence only as a pair of fingers poking into his mouth (and soon enough he learned to suck eagerly at those poking fingers in spite of the bitter taste)."

When she sees his manuscript copy of *Fast Cars*, she looks at him with disapproval, mixed with love; and Paul observes that "It was a maternal look." She praises his writing talent as a mother would a child and then feeds him again: "Her fingers were in his mouth suddenly, shockingly intimate, dirtily welcome. He sucked the capsules from between them and swallowed even before he could fumble the spilling glass of water to his mouth."

Eventually, memories of his mother and childhood and thoughts about Annie merge. He remembers a trip to the Boston Zoo and his empathy for the African bird doomed to die in its cage far away from its native land. Because he cried for the bird on the way home, his mother called him a "bawl-baby and a sissy." As he wills Annie to say more about what happened when she was on trial in Denver, Paul juxtaposes his feelings about Annie with his ambivalent feelings about his mother:

> "Come on," he muttered, his arm over his eyes—this was the way he thought best, the way he *imagined* best. His mother liked to tell Mr. Mulvaney on the other side of the fence what a marvellous imagination he had, so vivid, and what wonderful little stories he was always writing down (except, of course, she was calling him a sissy and a bawl-baby.). . . .
>
> *Annie Wilkes*
> *("He read at just three! Can you imagine!")*
> *That spirit of . . . of fan-love . . .*
> *("He's always writing things down, making things up.")*
> *Now I must rinse.*
> *("Africa. That bird came from.")*

Soon after, when Annie makes Paul burn *Fast Cars* (his dirty book with the offensive "effword" in it), she likens herself to a mother dutifully punishing a child she has caught being bad. And, when he refuses to light the match, she calls him "a very stubborn little boy."

Finally, when Paul escapes from his room the first time and thinks he hears Annie's car pulling up, he is filled with the greatest terror he had ever felt and an unmanning guilt. His terror reminds him of the time his mother returned home unexpectedly and caught him smoking when he was twelve: "the only incident in his life that came remotely close to this one in its desperate emotional quality." He becomes that twelve-year-old child again when Annie returns, and he begins to cry: "It was guilt he cried from, and he hated that most of all: in addition to everything else this monstrous woman had done to him, she had made him feel guilty as well. So he cried from guilt . . . but also from simple childish weariness."

FREUD AND CASTRATION ANXIETY

Paul's foot and thumbectomy, which terrorize him even more, are both figurative castrations. In his essay "The 'Uncanny,'" Freud states that "dismembered limbs, a severed head, a hand cut off at the wrist, [and] feet which dance by themselves" are associated with the "castration-complex." He also connects fear of the Sand-man with figurative castration in E.T.A. Hoffman's story "The Sand-Man." Hoffman's protagonist is terrified by his nurse's description of the Sand-Man: "a wicked man who comes when children won't go to bed, and throws handfuls of sand in their eyes so that they jump out of their heads all bleeding." Early in *Misery*, Annie becomes the sand-man, a phallic mother who threatens to castrate Paul. Paul dreams that Annie comes into his room dressed as the heroine of his novels, a basket over her arm: "She reached in [the basket] and took out a handful of something and flung it into the face of the . . . sleeping Paul Sheldon. It was sand, he saw—this was Annie Wilkes pretending to be Misery Chastain pretending to be the sandman. Sand*woman*. Then he saw that . . . Paul Sheldon's face had turned a ghastly white as soon as the sand struck it and fear jerked him out of the dream and into the bedroom, where Annie Wilkes was standing over him." He recalls this dream later—while reading the obituaries of Annie's murder victims in her scrapbook. He again has a vision of Annie holding a basket over her arm flinging sand into "upturned faces. . . . This was not the soothing sand of sleep but poisoned sand. It was killing them."

Castration is also *consciously* in both Paul's and Annie's mind. When he finds that Annie's phone does not work, for example, he concludes that she had castrated it; drugged from his first pre-op shot, Paul is "utterly sure that she meant to pull the knife from the wall and castrate him with it"; and when he contemplates the horror of the loss of his thumb, he thinks of how much worse it could have been: "It could have been [my] penis, for instance. And I only have one of those." Finally, Annie admits that she *had* considered cutting off his "man-gland."

After Paul is mutilated, his writer's block and passivity also suggest that he has become a eunuch: "He seemed to have lost some vital ingredient, and the mix had become a lot less potent as a result." Annie Wilkes is not the most terrifying part of *Misery*, but the poor, poor thing that Paul becomes mentally. When he sees the state trooper in Annie's driveway, for example, Paul is at first unable to respond:

> Nothing which had gone before—except perhaps for the moment when he realized that, although his left leg was moving, his left foot was staying put—was as terrible as the hell of this immobility. . . . He knew how constantly he had been terrorized, but did he know how much of his own subjective reality, once so strong he had taken it for granted, had been erased?
>
> He knew one thing with some certainty—a lot more was wrong with him than paralysis of the tongue. . . . The truth of everything was so simple in its horridness; so dreadfully simple. He was dying by inches, but dying that way wasn't as bad as he'd already feared. But he was also *fading*, and that was an awful thing because it was moronic.

A PARODY OF MARRIAGE

Annie and Paul's relationship parodies a marital one as well as a parental one. Abandoned by her husband, and "retired" from her nursing career, Annie's "relationship" with Paul fills a void in her empty life. As Paul lies helpless in bed when he first regains consciousness and then later as he writes his novel in the wheelchair, Annie often does traditionally female chores in the background. She prepares meals, washes dishes, vacuums, dusts, and washes the floors. By keeping

Paul prisoner, she is living out a fantasy through escape in his fiction and through their relationship. Paul even refers to himself as Scheherazade, both the storyteller and the wife of the king in *Arabian Nights*. Early in April, before the rains begin, she behaves like a happy housewife: "Annie . . . had never been in better spirits than she was during that sunny early-spring week. She cleaned; she cooked ambitious meals . . . , each afternoon she bundled Paul up in a huge blanket, jammed a green hunting cap on his head, and rolled him out onto the back porch."

The two horrifying dismemberments are ways of crippling Paul to keep him with her, but more importantly to reestablish her power over him. They also can be seen as representations of the primal scene. Awakening to find himself drugged by his first pre-op shot, Paul is disoriented, and Annie plays the coquette: "I *see* you, Paul . . . those blue eyes. Did I ever tell you what lovely blue eyes you have? But I suppose other women have—women who were much prettier than I am, and much bolder about their affections, as well." After she tells him about her former lover Pomeroy, she confesses that she began loving Paul because he wrote such wonderful stories; but her love for him changed. She began to love the rest of him because he is unlike other writers who drink and whore and shoot dope. Love notwithstanding, Annie wields the axe, an act suggestive of a much more violent rape than the earlier ones:

> The axe came whistling down and buried itself in Paul Sheldon's left leg just above the ankle. Pain exploded up his body in a gigantic bolt. Dark-red blood splattered across her face like Indian warpaint. It splattered the wall. He heard the blade squeal against bone as she wrenched it free. He looked unbelievably down at himself. The sheet was turning red. He saw his toes wriggling. Then he saw her raising the dripping axe again. Her hair had fallen free of its pins and hung around her blank face.

> He tried to pull back in spite of the pain in his leg and knee and realized that his leg was moving but his foot wasn't. All he was doing was widening the axe-slash, making it open like a mouth. He had time enough to realize his foot was now only held on his leg by the meat of his calf before the blade came down again, directly into the gash, shearing through the rest of his leg and burying itself deep in the mattress.

The dripping axe is most obviously phallic as it repeatedly hits the foot; and the cut, which opens like a mouth and bleeds, is suggestive of the vagina. The bloody mattress, of course, suggests loss of virginity. Even Annie's loosened hair makes her somewhat sensual, hinting at erotic pleasure in her sadism.

The thumbectomy also has sexual undertones. First she plugs the knife into the outlet by his wheelchair. Then there is a phallic injection. As the knife saws "rapidly back and forth in the air the Betadine flew in a spray of maroon droplets . . . and in the end of course there had been much redder droplets spraying into the air as well." This time the blood suggests the release of semen during climax. And "as the humming, vibrating blade sank into the soft web of flesh between the soon-to-be-defunct thumb and his first finger," Annie metaphorically climaxes also. Words of love once again are juxtaposed to the violent act; she assures Paul in her "this-hurts-Mother-more-than-it-hurts-Paulie voice that she loved him."

WRITING AND EROTICISM

Paul's writing, which he refers to as autoerotic, also satisfies Annie sexually: "But hadn't there been some sort of fuck," he thinks, "even of the driest variety? Because once he started again. . . . Well, she wouldn't interrupt him while he was working, but she would take each day's output as soon as he was done, ostensibly to fill in the missing letters, but actually—he knew this by now, just as sexually acute men know which dates will put out at the end of the evening and which will not—to get her fix. To get her *gotta*." For the *gotta*, he says, is "Nasty as a hand-job in a sleazy bar, fine as a fuck from the world's most talented call-girl." Note also that as he approaches the end of *Misery's Return*, he abandons the typewriter and writes with his Berol Black Warrior pencils, which Annie sharpens for him when he writes them dull. In her essay on Dickens and Freud's "The 'Uncanny'," Dianne Sadoff points out the connection between writing and the phallus: "the word 'pencil,' of course derives from Latin *penicillus*, which derives from the diminutive, *penis*, a tail. This common figure, the pen-as-phallus, represents the enabling power of writing to engender rendered life . . . art or writing may capture its subject's head [castration], may break the phallus [the dull points—Paul's dismemberment], but it restores the phallus as well; it repeats the enigma of castration and representation."

As Paul learns about Annie's mental state and grows to understand her, their relationship changes and evolves, again a parody of a marital one. He observes first her bouts of catatonia, and he imagines that her thoughts become as he had imagined her physical self—"solid, fibrous, unchannelled, with no places of hiatus." Paul becomes "suddenly very scared" when Annie slides into her depressive period in which she both gorges and abuses herself. When he escapes from his room the second time, Paul examines the remains of one of Annie's feasts: *"That was what I saw on her housecoat. The stuff she was eating. And what was on her breath.* His image of Annie as Piltdown woman recurred. He saw her sitting in here and scooping ice-cream into her mouth, or maybe handfuls of half-congealed chicken gravy with a Pepsi chaser, simply eating and drinking in a deep depressed haze."

ANNIE AS VICTIM

After she discusses killing the state trooper, Paul sees craziness in Annie's grin and "something else as well. . . . He sees conscious evil in it—a demon capering behind her eyes." But Annie is not an actual monster, or a cannibal, or a vampire, or a centaur, or the Bourka Bee-Goddess. The real Annie—the inside Annie . . . with all her masks put aside is a "crazy lady," curiously pathetic as well as frightening. In her depressive state, in fact, she seems as much a victim as Paul: "The flesh of her face, which had previously seemed so fearsomely solid, now hung like lifeless dough. Her eyes were blanks. She had dressed, but her skirt was on inside out. There were more weals on her flesh, more food splattered on her clothes. When she moved, they exhaled too many different aromas for Paul to count. Nearly one whole arm of her cardigan sweater was soaked with a half-dried substance that smelled like gravy." She may be a symbolic vampire/cannibal who is gorging herself, but she is certainly not *gaining* in power and strength. She goes to her "Laughing Place" to relieve herself of her painful depression; but while she is there, mostly she screams.

After Paul reads Annie's memory book of obituaries of her victims, he even empathizes with her. Annie divides all the people in the world into "three groups: brats, poor poor things [who had to be killed to relieve them from their misery] and Annie." Psychotic Annie Wilkes has murdered more than thirty people, including her own father, but she is also a poor poor thing. Annie is a victim of her manic-depressive cycles, her compulsion to rid the world of brats and to end the misery of poor poor things (rats in traps). She is a lonely loser whose major gratification in life is in reading popular fiction. Paul actually feels sorry for her when the reporters and police harass her. And when Annie is excited about reading the end of *Misery's Return*, and apologizes for the typewriter, he sees in her the "woman she might have been if her upbringing had been right or the drugs squirted out by all the funny little glands inside her had been less wrong. Or both."

ANOTHER SEXUAL ROLE REVERSAL

But just as the dull points of his pencils become sharp again, Paul finally overcomes Annie, ironically in an Annie-like fashion. He "rapes" and "sodomizes" her, and then he kills his vampire-captor with a typewriter rather than a stake. After he pretends to burn the novel she made him write (refusing her her sexual gratification at knowing how it ends), he drops the typewriter, the symbol of his forced prostitution, on her back. Then he knocks the board he used for a desk aside, "push[es] himself up and totter[s] *erect* on his right foot," while Annie lies "*writhing*" and "*moaning*" on the floor. Finally, in an attempt to assert his lost manhood, he falls on top of her. Once again, the sexual implications of the power struggle are implicit:

> The flames were going out around them but he could still feel savage heat coming off the twisting, heaving mound beneath him, and knew that at least some of her sweater and brassiere must be cooked onto her body. He felt no sympathy at all.

> She tried to buck him off. He held on, and now he was lying squarely on top of her like a man who means to commit a rape, his face almost on hers; his right hand groped, knowing exactly what it was looking for.

Like the earlier ones, this rape is also juxtaposed to Annie's gluttony. Paul forces Annie to eat his member and their baby. He stuffs page after page of the manuscript into her "gaping, screaming mouth. . . . She bucked and writhed under him. The salt-dome of his left knee whammed the floor and there was excruciating pain, but he stayed on top of her. ('I'm gonna rape you, all right, Annie. I'm gonna rape you because all I can do is the worst I can do. So suck my book. Suck my book. Suck on it until you . . . CHOKE'). He crumpled the wet paper with a convulsive closing jerk of his fist and slammed it into her mouth, driving the half-charred first bunch further down." Annie doesn't give up the sexual-power struggle easily, though. Despite her fractured skull, the severe burns, and the paper in her throat, she manages to crawl after Paul and to collapse on top of *him*, forcing him to "work his way out from her like a man burrowing his way out of a snowslide."

He locks himself into the bathroom and passes out, but when he awakens, his castration-complex returns. He imagines Annie is standing outside the door, axe in her hands, planning to "amputate his head." Fortunately, she dies before she can get back to him with the chainsaw.

Despite this victory, back in New York nine months later, Paul remains a poor poor thing haunted by the undead monster who appears in his apartment in her nurse's uniform, axe in hand, to decapitate/castrate him in his fantasy. He is lonely, crippled, and still in pain He substitutes bourbon for what she fed him—the Annie-dope he craves; and unable to write, he is still being terrorized by Annie Wilkes: "In his dreams and waking fantasies, he dug her up again and again. You couldn't kill the goddess. Temporarily dope her with bourbon, maybe, but that was all." The ending suggests that Paul defeats Annie again when he overcomes his writer's block, but what will happen when the hole in the paper disappears?

PAUL SHELDON AND STEPHEN KING

Paul Sheldon's fate is especially frightening because it reflects fears of both his creator King and of the reading public. When asked in a *Playboy* interview whether he "ever fears that things are going just *too* well . . . and that suddenly some malign cosmic force is going to snatch it all away," King responded: "I don't fear it, I *know* it. There's no way some disaster or illness or other cataclysmic affliction isn't already lurking in wait for me down the road. Things never get better, you know; they only get worse. And . . . we are rewarded only moderately for being good, but our transgressions are penalized with absurd severity." That is precisely what happens to Paul Sheldon. He freed himself from writing *Misery* novels by killing off his heroine, and he spent two years writing *Fast Cars*, a serious novel. But he transgressed by ordering a second bottle of Dom Perignon and setting off on a "Grand Odyssey to Somewhere." And everything was snatched away when he wrecked his car, and he was "saved" by Annie Wilkes.

Pet Sematary and the Paradox of Death

Douglas E. Winter

For many readers and scholars, *Pet Sematary* is Stephen King's most terrifying novel. It depicts the destruction of the all-American Creed family by the forces of evil loosed from the Micmac burial grounds. King has admitted frightening himself with the novel (which he called "a nasty book"), and later expressed regret that he had published it. *Pet Sematary* has literary forebears in Mary Shelley's *Frankenstein* and W.W. Jacobs's "The Monkey's Paw." Dr. Louis Creed's ill-fated attempts to resurrect first the family cat Church, then, tragically, his small son Gage, by burying the bodies in the haunted Indian cemetery, result in the emergence of vicious monsters that reanimate the shells of the dead. But King's reworking of the Prometheus myth— of a man trying to wrest the power of life and death from the gods—is cast in strikingly contemporary, American terms. Like many middle-class American families in the 1980s, the Creeds flee the stresses of urban life for the small-town, pastoral setting of Ludlow, Maine. But as is often the case with King's seemingly storybook-perfect Maine towns, beneath the dreamscape lies a nightmare.

In the following selection, leading King critic Douglas E. Winter discusses the novel's origins in the author's own family experiences and how it earned a reputation as King's most frightening novel even before its publication. Winter is equally interested in *Pet Sematary*'s mature exploration of death's paradoxical mystery and inevitability. For Winter, King's craft in leading Louis Creed (and the reader with him) toward an unrelenting abyss, beyond hope or redemption, elevates *Pet Sematary* to the level of art.

> Douglas E. Winter is a novelist and the editor of several important anthologies of modern horror fiction.

Rumors have circulated about a Stephen King novel that was too frightening to be published. The prospect was certainly enticing: what kind of story could possibly prove so terrifying as to stay the hand of the best-selling writer of horror fiction of all time? And although the truth of the matter proves something decidedly different, the novel in question, *Pet Sematary* (1983), doubtless satisfies any reader's expectations of the delicious fear that King's formidable talent can evoke.

THE ORIGINS OF KING'S IDEA FOR THE NOVEL

In early 1979, King was serving as writer-in-residence at his *alma mater*, the University of Maine at Orono, teaching courses that served as the proving grounds for much of *Danse Macabre*. His rented house, in nearby Orrington, bordered a major truck route—a road that seemed to consume stray dogs and cats; in the woods behind the house, up a small hill, local children had created an informal pet cemetery. One day, a neighbor called to inform King that a passing truck had killed his daughter's cat, Smucky. King was faced with the disconcerting tasks of burying the cat in the pet cemetery and then explaining to his daughter what had happened:

> *My impulse was to tell her that I hadn't seen him around; but [my wife] Tabby said no, that she had to have that experience. So I told her, and she cried and cried. . . .*

> *The next day . . . we heard her out in the garage. She was in there, jumping up and down, popping these plastic packing sheets and saying, "Let God have His own cat. I want my cat. I want my cat."*

It was on the third day after the burial, he reports rather ominously, that the idea for a novel came to him. What would happen, King wondered, if a young family were to lose their daughter's cat to a passing truck, and the father, rather than tell his daughter, were to bury the cat on a remote plot of land—something like a pet cemetery. And what would happen if the cat were to return the next day, alive but fundamentally different—fundamentally *wrong*. And then, if that family's two-year-old son were to fall victim to another passing truck. . . . The book would be a conscious retelling of W.W. Jacobs' "The Monkey's Paw" (1902), that enduring short story about parents who literally wish their son back from the dead:

> *When ideas come, they don't arrive with trumpets. They are quiet—there is no drama involved. I can remember crossing the road, and thinking that the cat had been killed in the road . . . and [I thought], what if a kid died in that road? And we had had this experience with Owen running toward the road, where I had just grabbed him and pulled him back. And the two things just came together—on one side of this two-lane highway was the idea of what if the cat came back, and on the other side of the highway was what if the kid came back—so that when I reached the other side, I had been galvanized by the idea, but not in any melodramatic way. I knew immediately that it was a novel.*

That night King dreamed of a reanimated corpse walking up and down the road outside of the house, he began to think about funerals, the modern customs surrounding death and burial: "I said to myself, 'If anybody else wanted to write about that, people would say that he's really morbid.' But I've got a reputation. I'm like a girl of easy virtue—one more won't hurt."

PET SEMATARY'S FIRST DRAFT

But it did hurt. When King completed the first draft in May of 1979, the book he had come to call *Pet Sematary* (using a child's spelling) was put away. He did not wish to work on it further; the novel was tinged with anxieties about his youngest child, who it had been feared—fortunately, incorrectly—was hydrocephalic, and his difficulties in coming to grips with the implications of the death of a child:

> *The book started off as a lark, but it didn't finish up that way. It stopped being a lark when I realized that the kid would have to die—and that I had never had to deal with the consequences of death on a rational level.*
>
> *I have always been aware of the things that I didn't want to write about. The death of a child is one—and the death of Tad Trenton at the end of* Cujo *was bad enough, but there I didn't have to deal with the aftermath. And I have always shied away from the entire funeral process—the aftermath of death. The funeral parlors, the burial, the grief, and, particularly where you are dealing with the death of a healthy child, the guilt—the feeling that you are somehow at fault. And for me, it was like looking through a window into something that could be.*
>
> *I decided that, if I was going to write this book, perhaps it would be good for me—in the Calvinist sense—to go through with it, to find out everything, and to see what would happen.*
>
> *But in trying to cope with these things, the book ceased being a novel to me, and became instead a gloomy exercise, like an endless marathon run. It never left my mind; it never ceased to trouble me. I was trying to teach school, and the boy was always there, the funeral home was always there, the mortician's room was always there.*
>
> *And when I finished, I put the book in a drawer.*

Prepublication Rumors

In a television interview, King unwittingly sparked rumors that the book was too frightening to be published:

> *It was the first time I had ever been asked the question:*

> *"Did you ever write anything too horrible to be published?"*
> *And this book came immediately to mind; Tabby had fin-*
> *ished reading it in tears, and I thought it was a nasty*
> *book—I still think that it is a nasty book. Twenty years ago,*
> Pet Sematary *would not have been a publishable novel . . .*
> *because of its subject matter and theme. Maybe I don't have*
> *the guts for that end of the business of horror fiction—for*
> *the final truths.*

Whether the book would have been published entirely of King's volition is now a moot question. Fate intervened, in the form of a contractual dispute with his former hardcover publisher, Doubleday. Rewritten in 1982, *Pet Sematary* appeared in 1983 only as ransom for substantial money, earned by King's early novels, that had been withheld from him. He allowed Doubleday, in its promotion of the book, to perpetuate the myth that had grown up around the novel; but he would not assist in the promotion of *Pet Sematary* or, indeed, talk with anyone about the book, save for the single interview on which this [essay] is based:

> *About a year after the original manuscript was finished,*
> *one of my teachers, a lady who I loved almost as much as I*
> *loved my mother, died. And she had left a request that I*
> *read from* Proverbs *at her funeral. And although by then I*
> *was considered a "public figure," and I had spoken often on*
> *television and in public, I almost lost it. My voice was this*
> *sort of wild trembling and I could feel my pulse in my col-*
> *lar, the way you do when your tie is too tight, and the whole*
> *thing just seemed to come in on me and suffocate me.*
>
> *And it was all part of this book—because you open these*
> *doors; and that [is] why I don't want to talk about this book.*
>
> *So it hurts me to talk about it; it hurts me to think about it.*
> Pet Sematary *is the one book that I haven't reread—I never*
> *want to go back there again, because it is a* real *cemetery.*

Precisely because of King's closeness to its subject matter,

Pet Sematary is one of the most vivid, powerful, and disturbing tales he has written. His hallmarks—effortless, colloquial prose, and an unerring instinct for the visceral—are in evidence throughout, but this novel succeeds because of King's ability to produce characters so familiar that they may as well have lived next door for years.

Louis Creed, a young physician, has moved his family from Chicago to Ludlow, Maine (a thinly disguised Orrington), where he will manage a university infirmary. Creed is the most hardheaded of rationalists: "He had pronounced two dozen people dead in his career and had never once felt the passage of a soul." His wife, Rachel, on the other hand, shrinks with preternatural fear from the very thought of death—as a child, she had witnessed the final agonies of a sister ravaged by spinal meningitis and, much as Stephen King had been alone when he discovered his grandmother's death, was left alone by her parents on the day that her sister died. When an elderly Downeaster, Jud Crandall, takes the Creeds to visit the "Pet Sematary" in the woods behind their rented house, their six-year-old daughter, Ellie, immediately fears for the life of her cat, Winston Churchill (wryly nicknamed "Church"):

> [Creed] held her and rocked her, believing, rightly or wrongly, that Ellie wept for the very intractability of death, its imperviousness to argument or to a little girl's tears; that she wept over its cruel unpredictability; and that she wept because of the human being's wonderful, deadly ability to translate symbols into conclusions that were either fine and noble or blackly terrifying. If all those animals had died and been buried, then Church could die . . . and be buried; and if that could happen to Church, it could happen to her mother, her father, her baby brother. To herself, Death was a vague idea; the Pet Sematary was real.

The reality of the Pet Sematary soon invades the life of Louis Creed. On his first day at work, a student dies in his

arms after uttering a sybilic warning: "It's not the real cemetery." That night, Creed's sleep is interrupted by an appari-
tion of the dead student, which leads him back to the Pet Sematary: "Don't go beyond, no matter how much you feel you
need to," it says. "The barrier was not made to be broken."

THE STRUGGLE WITH DEATH

Death follows death, as inexorably as a falling column of
dominoes; and it strikes next in the Creed household. Ful-
filling Ellie's dark apprehension at the sight of the Pet Sematary, Church is killed by a passing truck. King named Ellie's cat with a purpose; in the death of Church, he signals
that the issue at the heart of *Pet Sematary* is that of the rational being's struggle with modern death—death without
God, death without hope of salvation.

Aware of the pain that Church's death will cause Ellie, Jud
Crandall initiates Creed into the secret that lies *beyond* the
Pet Sematary—an ancient burial ground long abandoned by
Indians. Creed is reminded of Stonehenge; there is a sensation of incredible age in the spiraling arrangement of cairns,
a sensation reinforced when Crandall begins to speak of Indian legends of the Wendigo. He directs Creed to bury the
cat there; and the cat, just like in the nursery rhyme, returns
the very next day—awkward, loathsome to touch, stinking
of sour earth, but *alive*—setting the stage for a haunting
moral dilemma: whether, regardless of the cost, death should
be cheated.

When two-year-old Gage, the book's most endearing
character, is killed by another passing truck, Louis Creed's
mourning is not that of a sentimental Pietà, but the driven
ambition of a Faust. Should he take the corpse of his son beyond the Pet Sematary? "You do it because it gets hold of
you," Crandall warns. "You do it because that burial place is
a secret place, and you want to share the secret. . . . You make
up reasons . . . they seem like good reasons . . . but mostly
you do it because you want to."

In *Cujo*, for which *Pet Sematary* is a thematic bookend, the rabid dog becomes a symbol of nature, a literal embodiment of King's naturalistic stance—"free will was not a factor." In *Pet Sematary*, he invokes a time-honored symbol of nature, the Wendigo. This malevolent spirit-being of north country Indian folklore, an anthropomorphization of the cold and forbidding northern environment, is said to have polluted the once-hallowed burial ground, disturbing the sleep of the dead. In the symbol of the Wendigo, whose overshadowing presence Creed may have glimpsed on his journey to bury Gage, King confirms the purpose of the fakir in "The Monkey's Paw": "He wanted to show that fate ruled people's lives, and that those who interfered with it did so to their sorrow." Which, King notes, "I suppose is a comfort."

THE FAILURE OF REASON AGAINST NATURE

Pet Sematary is, then, an inward-looking narrative, focused upon the question of moral responsibility for interference with the natural order. Creed, like Church, is named with intention; his creed—rationality—is the flaw that pushes him along the path to destruction. He has apparently acquired the ultimate skill of his profession as a physician—the ability to return the dead to life—and he cannot help but use it. King comments:

> *He never ceases to be the rational man. Everything is plotted out—this is what can happen, this is what can't happen. But nothing that he thinks can happen is eventually what does happen.*

> *The book is very Christian in that sense, because it is a book about what happens when you attempt miracles without informing them with any sense of real soul. When you attempt mechanistic miracles—abracadabra, pigeon and pie, the monkey's paw—you destroy everything.*

In the rational order of things, fathers do not bury their sons. The death of a child is the ultimate horror of every parent, an outrage against humanity; and the reanimated Gage is precisely that horror made flesh, savaging and literally eating away at his mourning family. The lesson King offers is that which he reluctantly taught his daughter when her cat died—the lesson that Dick Hallorann, the surrogate father of *The Shining*, taught Danny Torrance: "You grieve for your daddy. . . . That's what a good son has to do. But see that you get on. That's your job in this hard world, to keep your love alive and see that you get on, no matter what. Pull your act together and just go on." Death is a part of the natural order of things; and, as another surrogate father, Jud Crandall, tells Louis Creed: "Sometimes dead is better."

Creed thus finds no consolation in his acts—only an abyss, the dark hole of death. In acceptance of death, he could have kept his love alive through memories of his son, but the "miracles" from beyond the Pet Sematary only confirm his rationalist world view, crushing his memories through a vision of a mindless chaos—indeed, malevolence—awaiting at the end of life. Yet he returns again to the burial ground with the body of his wife, and as the novel ends, waits alone for her return. "What this novel says," King holds, "is that it is worth *everything*, even your own soul." ("But would you do it?" I ask him. "Knowing what Louis Creed knows at the end of the book, would you do it?" He smiles for a moment, then looks at me with confident self-knowledge: "No.")

CREED'S TRAGIC QUEST

Louis Creed's quest is carried out in secrecy—he arrogates the power over death unto himself, his rational mind in triumph over the emotion of his heart; as Jud Crandall observes:

> "[T]he things that are in a man's heart . . . are secret things. Women are supposed to be the ones good at keeping secrets, and I guess they do keep a few, but any woman who knows anything at all would tell you she has never really seen into any man's heart. The soil of a man's heart is

> *stonier, Louis—like the soil up there in the old Micmac*
> *burying ground. Bedrock's close. A man grows what he can*
> *. . . and he tends it."*

Secrets are the dark undercurrent of *Pet Sematary:* not simply the secrets that divide man and woman, husband and wife—such as the moments of unfaithfulness to their wives that both Creed and Crandall hold locked in their stony hearts; or the secrets of the mortician's room, to whose door King takes us, yet whose contents we never see; or, of course, the secrets of the burial place that lies beyond the Pet Sematary. The ultimate secret, the impenetrable bedrock beneath the stony soil, is that of death, which King aptly symbolizes as Oz the Great and Terrible ("Tewwible," in the words of Rachel Creed's dying sister, again a child's usage)—the unknowable overlord whose masquerade we cannot pierce . . . until we die.

"*Death is a mystery, and burial is a secret,*" King tells us here, and in those few words pinpoints the key to his popularity and the abiding lure of the uncanny for writers and readers alike. As a committed writer of horror fiction, Stephen King works, by choice, in a *genre* responsible for countless films and paperback potboilers whose sole concern is the shock value of make-believe mayhem. But as *Pet Sematary* makes clear, the horror story—at its most penetrating, important moments, those of the immaculate clarity of insight which we call art—is not about make-believe at all. It is a literature whose essence is our single certainty—that, in Hamlet's words, "all that live must die."

KING AND THE EXPLORATION OF DEATH

What lies in wait for us, down the dark hole of death?

Do the dead sing?

We began this exploration of the night journeys of Stephen King with the story of Stella Flanders [the heroine of King's short story "The Reach"], which asked the question explicitly—and answered in the affirmative. For although death awaits Stella Flanders at the far side of the Reach, it is a gentle, lovely death—hand-in-hand with friends who have passed before her, singing hymns of grace. Her journey through darkness, like the journeys of *The Stand*, *The Dead Zone*, and *Firestarter*, emerges to light, renewing Doctor Van Helsing's observation in *Dracula:* "We must go through bitter waters before we taste the sweet." Her journey's end is indeed different from that of the "small animals" down the dark hole of *Cujo*, and from the song greeting Carrie White at the finale of *Carrie:* "that last lighted thought carried swiftly down the black tunnel of eternity, followed by the blank, idiot hum of prosaic electricity." Or from the fates of Father Callahan in *'Salem's Lot* and David Drayton in "The Mist," doomed as eternal fugitives in night journeys that may never end.

As these disparate destinies suggest, the question—"Do the dead sing?"—must go unanswered, at least for the moment. Like Louis Creed, waiting for his wife's return from beyond the Pet Sematary, and like Stella Flanders' son, left on this side of the Reach, we can only conjecture until it is our time to know. "We fall from womb to tomb, from one blackness toward another," King has written, " remembering little of the one and knowing nothing of the other . . . except through faith." But in the tale of horror, we may experience that fall, the journey into night, yet live again; thus in King's "The Last Rung on the Ladder," two Nebraska farm children play a game of falling from the loft of a barn into stacks of new-mown hay below—an apt metaphor for the horror story: "[Y]ou'd come to rest in that smell of reborn summer with your stomach left behind you way up there in the air, and you'd feel . . . well, you'd feel like Lazarus must have felt . . . fresh and new, like a baby." Always lurking, whether sought or simply found in these night journeys, is the other side of our self and our existence—the elusive phantom of life. And the darkness, the night, the eternal negation of the grave, give us access to truths that we might not otherwise obtain. In "Ad Astram," William Faulkner wrote a fitting credo for horror fiction: "A man sees further looking out of the dark upon the light than a man does in the light and looking out upon the light."

Death, destruction, and destiny await us all at the end of the journey—in life as in horror fiction. And the writer of horror stories serves as the boatman who ferries people across that Reach known as the River Styx—offering us a full dress rehearsal of death, while returning us momentarily to our youth. The Reach *was* wider in those days. And even as we read these words, the Reach is shortening, and the future beckons us even as the ghosts of our past are calling us home. In the horror fiction of Stephen King, we can embark upon the night journey, make the descent down the dark hole, cross that narrowing Reach, and return again in safety to the surface—to the near shore of the river of death.

For our boatman has a master's hand.

FOR FURTHER RESEARCH

Works by Stephen King

Carrie. New York: Doubleday, 1974.

'Salem's Lot. New York: Doubleday, 1975.

The Shining. New York: Doubleday, 1977.

Night Shift. New York: Doubleday, 1978.

The Stand. New York: Doubleday, 1978.

The Dead Zone. New York: Viking, 1979.

Firestarter. New York: Viking, 1980.

Danse Macabre. New York: Everest House, 1981.

Cujo. New York: Viking, 1981.

Creepshow. New York: New American Library, 1982.

Different Seasons. New York: Viking, 1982.

The Dark Tower: The Gunslinger. West Kingston, RI: Donald M. Grant, 1982.

Christine. New York: Viking, 1983.

Pet Sematary. New York: Doubleday, 1983.

The Talisman (written with Peter Straub). New York: Viking, 1984.

Cycle of the Werewolf (illustrated by Berni Wrightson). Westland, MI: Land of Enchantment, 1984.

Thinner [published under the pseudonym Richard Bachman]. New York: New American Library, 1984.

Skeleton Crew. New York: Putnam, 1985.

The Bachman Books: Four Early Novels (Rage, The Long Walk,

The Running Man, Roadwork). New York: New American Library, 1985.

It. New York: Viking, 1986.

The Eyes of the Dragon. New York: Viking, 1987.

Misery. New York: Viking, 1987.

The Dark Tower: The Drawing of the Three. New York: New American Library, 1987.

The Tommyknockers. New York: Putnam, 1987.

Nightmares in the Sky: Gargoyles and Grotesques. New York: Viking, 1988.

The Dark Half. New York: Viking, 1989.

Four Past Midnight. New York: Viking, 1990.

The Stand. Revised and unexpurgated edition. New York: Doubleday, 1990.

The Dark Tower: The Wastelands. New York: New American Library, 1991.

Needful Things. New York: Viking, 1991.

Gerald's Game. New York: Viking, 1992.

Dolores Claiborne. New York: Viking, 1992.

Nightmares and Dreamscapes. New York: Viking, 1993.

Insomnia. New York: Viking, 1994.

Rose Madder. New York: Viking, 1995.

Desperation. New York: Viking, 1996.

The Regulators [Richard Bachman, pseud.]. New York: Viking, 1996.

The Green Mile (serial novel in six episodes). New York: Signet, 1996.

Wizard and Glass. West Kingston, RI: Donald M. Grant, 1997.

Bag of Bones. New York: Scribner, 1998.

The Girl Who Loved Tom Gordon. New York: Scribner, 1999.

Hearts in Atlantis. New York: Scribner, 1999.

Storm of the Century. New York: Pocket Books, 1999.

On Writing. New York: Scribner, 2000.

Dreamcatcher. New York: Scribner, 2001.

Black House (with Peter Straub). New York: Random House, 2001.

Everything's Eventual. New York: Scribner, 2002.

From a Buick 8. New York: Scribner, 2002.

Biography and Literary Criticism

Linda Badley, *Writing Horror and the Body: The Fiction of Stephen King, Clive Barker, and Anne Rice.* Westport, CT: Greenwood, 1996.

George Beahm, *Stephen King: America's Best-Loved Boogeyman.* Kansas City, MO: Andrews McMeel, 1995.

———, *The Stephen King Companion.* Kansas City, MO: Andrews McMeel, 1989.

———, *Stephen King: From A to Z.* Kansas City, MO: Andrews McMeel, 1998.

Harold Bloom, ed., *Stephen King: Modern Critical Views.* Philadelphia: Chelsea House, 1998.

Ray Browne and Gary Hoppenstand, eds., *The Gothic World of Stephen King: Landscape of Nightmares.* Bowling Green, OH: Bowling Green State University Popular Press, 1987.

Michael Collings, *The Films of Stephen King.* Mercer Island, WA: Starmont House, 1986.

———, *The Many Facets of Stephen King.* Mercer Island, WA: Starmont House, 1985.

———, *The Stephen King Phenomenon.* Mercer Island, WA: Starmont House, 1986.

Jonathan P. Davis, *Stephen King's America.* Bowling Green, OH: Bowling Green State University Popular Press, 1994.

Brian Docherty, ed., *American Horror Fiction: From Brockden Brown to Stephen King.* New York: St. Martin's, 1990.

Don Herron, ed., *Reign of Fear: Fiction and Films of Stephen King*. Los Angeles: Underwood-Miller, 1988.

Kathleeen Margaret Lant and Theresa Thompson, *Imagining the Worst: Stephen King and the Representation of Women*. Westport, CT: Greenwood Press, 1998.

Tony Magistrale, ed., *The Dark Descent: Essays Defining Stephen King's Horrorscape*. Westport, CT: Greenwood Press, 1992.

———, *Landscape of Fear: Stephen King's American Gothic*. Bowling Green, OII: Bowling Green State University Popular Press, 1988.

———, *The Moral Voyages of Stephen King*. Mercer Island, WA: Starmont House, 1989.

———, *Stephen King: The Second Decade*, Danse Macabre *to* The Dark Half. New York: Twayne, 1992.

Brenda Miller Power, Jeffrey D. Wilhelm, and Kelly Chandler, *Reading Stephen King: Issues of Censorship, Student Choice, and Popular Literature*. Urbana, IL: National Council of Teachers of English, 1997.

Joseph Reino, *Stephen King: The First Decade,* Carrie *to* Pet Sematary. Boston: Twayne, 1988.

Sharon A. Russell, *Stephen King: A Critical Companion*. Westport, CT: Greenwood, 1996.

Tim Underwood and Chuck Miller, eds., *Bare Bones: Conversations on Terror with Stephen King*. New York: McGraw-Hill, 1988.

———, *Fear Itself: The Horror Fiction of Stephen King*. San Francisco: Underwood-Miller, 1982.

———, *Feast of Fear: Conversations with Stephen King*. New York: Carroll and Graf, 1992.

———, *Kingdom of Fear: The World of Stephen King*. New York: New American Library, 1986.

Douglas E. Winter, *Stephen King: The Art of Darkness*. New York: New American Library, 1984.

INDEX